Open ai GPT for Python Developers

OPTIMIZING PERFORMANCE: FINE TUNING AND CUSTOMIZING GPT MODELS IN PYTHON

COPYRIGHTS

Contents

This book is not intended to be a substitute for professional advice. Always seek the advice of qualified professionals with any questions you may have regarding a specific technology, product, or service. The author and publisher do not endorse any specific product, technology, company, or service mentioned in this book

Chapter 1

Introduction to GPT and Its Customization Potential

OVERVIEW OF OPENAI GPT MODELS

Introduction to the Architecture and Capabilities of GPT Models

OpenAI's Generative Pretrained Transformer (GPT) models represent a significant advancement in natural language processing (NLP). The GPT models are built on the Transformer architecture, which was first introduced by Vaswani et al. in 2017. The Transformer architecture is a type of neural network designed to handle sequential data, such as text, by utilizing selfattention mechanisms. These mechanisms allow the model to weigh the importance of different words in a sentence relative to each other, enabling it to capture contextual relationships more effectively than previous models like RNNs (Recurrent Neural Networks) and LSTMs (Long ShortTerm Memory networks).

The GPT models are "pretrained" on massive datasets comprising diverse text from the internet. During pretraining, the model learns to predict the next word in a sentence, given the previous words. This process helps the model develop an understanding of grammar, facts about the world, reasoning abilities, and some level of problemsolving skills. After pretraining, GPT models can be finetuned on specific tasks with smaller datasets, making them highly versatile.

Key capabilities of GPT models include:

Text Generation: GPT can generate coherent and contextually relevant text based on a given prompt, making it useful for tasks like content creation, storytelling, and dialogue generation.

Text Completion: GPT can complete sentences or paragraphs when given a partial input, which is valuable for applications like code completion or email drafting.

Text Summarization: GPT can condense long articles or documents into shorter summaries, helping in content digestion and information retrieval.

Translation and Language Modeling: While not specialized in translation, GPT models can translate text between languages and predict the likelihood of a sequence of words, making them useful in various languagebased tasks.

Answering Questions: GPT can answer questions based on the input it receives, demonstrating an ability to perform certain reasoning tasks and retrieve information contextually.

KEY DIFFERENCES BETWEEN GPT2, GPT3, AND GPT4

As OpenAI has iterated on the GPT models, each version has brought improvements in size, capability, and performance. Understanding these differences is crucial for developers who want to optimize and customize these models for their specific use cases.

GPT2:

GPT2 was the first largescale version of the GPT model, consisting of 1.5 billion parameters. It marked a significant leap in NLP capabilities, demonstrating impressive performance on tasks like text generation, translation, and summarization without taskspecific training data. GPT2 was trained on a dataset of 8 million web pages, allowing it to generate highly coherent text.

However, it was also prone to producing content that, while fluent, could be factually incorrect or misleading. GPT2's architecture set the stage for larger models by proving that scaling up model size and training data could lead to better performance.

GPT3:

GPT3 expanded upon GPT2 significantly, with 175 billion parameters—over 100 times more than its predecessor. This vast increase in parameters allowed GPT3 to understand and generate more complex and nuanced text. It demonstrated the ability to perform tasks with zeroshot, oneshot, and fewshot learning, meaning it could generalize from very few examples. For instance, GPT3 could translate languages, perform arithmetic, write code, and even generate creative writing with minimal taskspecific examples. The sheer scale of GPT3 also made it more effective in capturing subtleties in language, leading to more contextually accurate outputs. However, the large model size also required substantial computational resources for deployment, making it less accessible for smallerscale applications.

GPT4:

GPT4, the latest in the series, builds on the foundation laid by GPT3 with further advancements in scale and refinement, though specific parameter details were not fully disclosed at the time of its release. GPT4 emphasizes improvements in reasoning, coherence, and factual accuracy. It can handle more complex queries and provide more reliable information, reducing the instances of generating misleading or incorrect text. GPT4 also introduces enhancements in finetuning and customization, making it easier for developers to adapt the model to specific tasks or industries. Another key feature of GPT4 is its better handling of ambiguous prompts, where it shows an improved ability to ask clarifying questions or offer multiple interpretations rather than making unwarranted assumptions.

Each iteration from GPT2 to GPT4 represents a significant leap in the capabilities and potential applications of generative models. GPT4, in particular, offers developers more tools and flexibility for customization, allowing for more precise and effective deployment in various domains, from conversational agents to content generation and beyond. Understanding these differences helps developers choose the right model and approach for their specific needs, especially when considering the tradeoffs between model size, performance, and resource requirements

IMPORTANCE OF FINETUNING AND CUSTOMIZATION

Why FineTuning GPT Models is Critical for Specific Tasks

While GPT models are pretrained on vast and diverse datasets, this general training does not necessarily make them ideal for every specific task or industry application. Finetuning is the process of taking a pretrained model like GPT and further training it on a smaller, more specific dataset relevant to the desired task. This additional training allows the model to adapt to specific vocabulary, style, and context that are critical for the task at hand, significantly enhancing its relevance and performance.

1. Adapting to DomainSpecific Language and Context:

In many specialized fields such as medicine, law, finance, or technology, the language used is often highly technical and nuanced. A generalpurpose GPT model might generate coherent text, but it could miss the mark in terms of domainspecific accuracy or fail to grasp the subtleties of specialized terminology. Finetuning allows the model to learn from domainspecific datasets, which can include proprietary information, jargon, or industry standards that are not wellrepresented in the broader internet text the model was initially trained on. For example, in the medical field, finetuning GPT on a dataset of medical research papers could improve its ability to generate accurate clinical summaries or assist in diagnosing conditions based on textual inputs.

2. Enhancing TaskSpecific Performance:

Different tasks require different capabilities from a language model. For example, customer support chatbots, content recommendation engines, automated report generation, and creative writing assistants each have unique requirements in terms of response style, accuracy, and creativity. Finetuning allows developers to calibrate the model's output to align closely with these taskspecific requirements. A customer support bot, for instance, might be finetuned to prioritize politeness and clarity, while a content generation model for a news outlet might be finetuned to ensure factual accuracy and journalistic tone.

3. Improving Model Efficiency and Resource Use:

Generalpurpose models like GPT3 and GPT4 are designed to be highly flexible, capable of handling a wide range of tasks with minimal adjustments. However, this flexibility comes at the cost of efficiency. Without finetuning, a GPT model might require more computational resources to produce accurate results, as it has to process a broader range of possibilities and interpretations. Finetuning streamlines this process by narrowing the model's focus, making it more efficient in generating the desired outputs. This reduction in computational overhead can lead to faster response times and lower costs, which is particularly important in realtime applications or environments with limited resources.

4. Addressing Ethical and Bias Concerns:

Pretrained models often reflect the biases present in the data they were trained on, which can lead to problematic or biased outputs. Finetuning offers an opportunity to correct or mitigate these biases by training the model on carefully curated datasets that emphasize fairness, inclusivity, and ethical considerations. This is especially crucial in applications that involve sensitive or highstakes decisionmaking, such as in the legal or hiring sectors, where biased outputs could have serious consequences.

5. Personalization and Brand Consistency:

For businesses and organizations, maintaining a consistent brand voice is crucial. Finetuning allows a GPT model to align closely with the brand's tone, style, and messaging guidelines. This customization is not only about avoiding errors but also about ensuring that every interaction—whether it's an email response, a chatbot conversation, or generated content—reflects the brand's identity. By finetuning the model on companyspecific data, including past communications, marketing materials, and product descriptions, businesses can ensure that the outputs are not only accurate but also onbrand.

BENEFITS OF CUSTOMIZATION FOR IMPROVING ACCURACY AND PERFORMANCE

1. Increased Relevance and Accuracy:

Customizing GPT models through finetuning allows them to produce more relevant and accurate outputs. By training the model on specific datasets that reflect the context, terminology, and style of the intended application, developers can significantly improve the accuracy of the generated text. For instance, a legal assistant model finetuned on legal documents will be more likely to generate correct legal language and references, reducing the risk of errors that could arise from using a generalpurpose model.

2. Enhanced User Experience:

Finetuning can dramatically improve the user experience by ensuring that the model's responses are tailored to the user's needs and expectations. For example, in a customer service application, finetuning can help the model better understand common customer queries and provide more accurate and helpful responses. This leads to higher satisfaction rates, as users receive answers that are not only accurate but also contextually appropriate and aligned with the company's service standards.

3. Flexibility and Adaptability:

Customization through finetuning allows GPT models to be adapted to a wide range of tasks and environments. This flexibility is crucial in dynamic fields where the requirements and challenges can change rapidly. For instance, in financial markets, where conditions can shift quickly, a finetuned model can be updated with the latest market data to provide accurate analysis and predictions. This adaptability makes finetuning an essential tool for businesses and developers who need to keep pace with evolving demands.

4. Better Handling of Complex Tasks:

Some tasks require a deep understanding of context, multiple layers of reasoning, or the ability to synthesize information from various sources. Finetuning enables GPT models to handle these complex tasks more effectively by training them on datasets that specifically prepare them for the intricacies of the task. For example, a model finetuned on technical manuals and product specifications might be better equipped to provide detailed technical support or generate complex documentation, compared to a generalpurpose model.

5. Improved ROI on AI Investments:

Investing in AI and machine learning technologies can be costly, particularly when deploying large models like GPT3 or GPT4. Finetuning and customization can help maximize the return on investment by ensuring that the model is highly effective for the specific tasks it is intended for. This targeted approach reduces the need for expensive retraining or additional resources to achieve desired outcomes, making AI investments more costeffective and sustainable over time.

In summary, finetuning and customization are not just optional enhancements but essential strategies for leveraging the full potential of GPT models. By tailoring these powerful tools to specific tasks and contexts, developers can significantly improve accuracy, efficiency, and user satisfaction, while also addressing ethical concerns and maintaining brand consistency. This approach ensures that the model is not only capable of performing general tasks but excels in delivering highquality, contextually relevant, and ethically sound outputs in its intended application.

USE CASES FOR CUSTOMIZED GPT MODELS

Examples of IndustrySpecific Applications and Benefits

Customized GPT models have become an invaluable asset across various industries, enabling organizations to harness the power of advanced natural language processing (NLP) tailored to their unique needs. The flexibility and adaptability of GPT models, when finetuned and customized, allow businesses to address specific challenges, streamline operations, and create new opportunities. Below are some prominent examples of how different industries are leveraging customized GPT models:

1. Healthcare and Medicine:

In the healthcare sector, GPT models can be finetuned to understand medical terminology, interpret clinical notes, and assist in patient care. For instance, a customized GPT model trained on electronic health records (EHRs) and medical literature can help in generating accurate medical reports, summarizing patient histories, and even suggesting potential diagnoses based on symptoms provided by patients. This capability can significantly reduce the administrative burden on healthcare professionals, allowing them to focus more on patient care.

Moreover, GPT models can be tailored to support telemedicine by providing accurate and contextaware responses to patient inquiries, guiding them through selfcare procedures, or advising on when to seek further medical attention. Finetuning the model on specific medical guidelines and patient interaction data ensures that the advice given is both relevant and reliable.

2. Finance and Investment:

In the financial sector, customized GPT models can assist in automating the generation of financial reports, analyzing market trends, and even predicting stock movements based on historical data. By finetuning a GPT model on financial news, market reports, and historical trading data, financial institutions can create a powerful tool that generates insights with a high degree of accuracy.

For example, a finetuned GPT model could analyze vast amounts of data to detect patterns that may indicate potential market shifts. It could then generate reports for analysts or provide realtime alerts to traders. Additionally, in customer service, GPT models can be customized to handle queries related to personal finance, investment advice, and transaction support, offering personalized and contextually appropriate responses that enhance customer satisfaction.

3. Legal Industry:

In the legal field, GPT models can be customized to assist with legal research, contract analysis, and even the drafting of legal documents. Finetuning the model on a database of legal cases, statutes, and regulations allows it to provide precise and contextually accurate legal information. Lawyers and legal professionals can use these models to quickly identify relevant case laws, draft contracts, and prepare legal briefs, significantly speeding up the legal research process.

For instance, a GPT model customized for contract review can automatically identify key clauses, highlight potential risks, and suggest amendments, saving legal teams hours of manual review. Additionally, such a model could be used in legal chatbots, providing clients with preliminary legal advice or answering frequently asked legal questions, thus reducing the workload on human legal professionals.

4. Ecommerce and Retail:

In the ecommerce sector, GPT models can be customized to enhance customer experience through personalized shopping assistants, product recommendations, and customer support chatbots. By finetuning a GPT model on product descriptions, customer reviews, and sales data, businesses can create a virtual shopping assistant that understands customer preferences and suggests products that align with their tastes and needs.

For example, a customized GPT model could analyze a customer's previous purchases and browsing history to provide personalized product recommendations. It could also engage with customers in realtime, answering questions about products, guiding them through the purchasing process, and even upselling related items. This level of personalization can lead to increased customer satisfaction, higher conversion rates, and ultimately, increased sales.

5. Education and ELearning:

In education, customized GPT models can be used to develop intelligent tutoring systems, generate educational content, and provide personalized learning experiences. Finetuning GPT models on educational materials, such as textbooks, lecture notes, and student feedback, enables them to understand the specific learning objectives and challenges students face.

For instance, an educational GPT model can generate custom quizzes, explain complex concepts in simpler terms, and even provide personalized study plans based on a student's progress and performance. Additionally, these models can be used to support teachers by automating administrative tasks like grading assignments and generating feedback, allowing educators to focus more on teaching.

CASE STUDIES ON CUSTOMIZED GPT IMPLEMENTATIONS

1. Healthcare: IBM's Watson for Oncology

IBM's Watson for Oncology is an example of a customized AI model that has been finetuned to assist oncologists in providing personalized cancer treatment options. By training the model on a vast amount of oncology research and clinical trial data, Watson can analyze a patient's medical records and suggest treatment options based on the latest evidence. This customization has led to significant improvements in treatment accuracy and has helped oncologists make more informed decisions, ultimately improving patient outcomes.

2. Finance: JPMorgan's COIN (Contract Intelligence)

JPMorgan Chase developed COIN, a customized AI model finetuned to analyze and interpret complex legal documents, particularly contracts. This model has been trained on thousands of legal documents, enabling it to identify and extract key information, assess risks, and even suggest changes to contracts. COIN has significantly reduced the time and cost associated with contract review, allowing the bank's legal teams to focus on more strategic tasks.

3. Ecommerce: Amazon's Personalized Shopping Recommendations

Amazon's recommendation system is one of the most wellknown examples of a customized AI model in ecommerce. By finetuning its algorithms on customer data, including browsing history, purchase history, and product reviews, Amazon can provide highly personalized product recommendations to its users. This customization has been a key factor in Amazon's success, driving customer engagement and boosting sales through tailored shopping experiences.

4. Legal: Ross Intelligence for Legal Research

Ross Intelligence is a legal research tool that uses a finetuned AI model to provide lawyers with precise legal research assistance. The model has been trained on a vast database of legal cases, statutes, and legal opinions, enabling it to answer complex legal questions, identify relevant case law, and provide citations. This customization has allowed Ross to become a valuable tool for legal professionals, reducing the time spent on research and increasing the accuracy of legal analysis.

5. Education: Duolingo's AIPowered Language Learning

Duolingo, a popular languagelearning platform, has implemented customized AI models to provide personalized language instruction to its users. By finetuning its models on linguistic data and user interactions, Duolingo can adapt its lessons to each user's learning style and progress. This customization has made Duolingo one of the most effective languagelearning tools, providing a tailored learning experience that adapts to the needs of each learner.

The potential for GPT models to be customized and finetuned for specific industry applications is immense. By adapting these models to particular domains and tasks, organizations can unlock significant benefits, including increased efficiency, enhanced accuracy, and improved user experiences. As these case studies demonstrate, the customization of GPT models is not just a theoretical possibility but a practical solution that is already transforming industries across the globe.

Chapter 2

Getting Started with FineTuning GPT Models

PREPARING THE PYTHON ENVIRONMENT

Setting Up Python for GPT FineTuning

To effectively finetune GPT models using Python, it's crucial to establish a wellconfigured development environment. This involves setting up Python itself, installing the necessary libraries, and ensuring that you have access to the hardware required for training. Below is a stepbystep guide to prepare your Python environment for finetuning GPT models:

1. Install Python:

Ensure you have Python 3.7 or higher installed on your system. Python can be downloaded from the official website [python.org](https://www.python.org/). When installing, make sure to check the option to add Python to your system PATH, which will allow you to use Python commands from the command line.

2. Create a Virtual Environment:

It's a good practice to use a virtual environment to manage dependencies for your project. This helps to avoid conflicts between different projects. You can create a virtual environment using the following commands:

```bash
Install virtualenv if not already installed

pip install virtualenv

Create a new virtual environment

virtualenv gptfinetuningenv

Activate the virtual environment

On Windows

gptfinetuningenv\Scripts\activate
```

On macOS/Linux

source gptfinetuningenv/bin/activate

```
```
```

3. Install Required Libraries:

With your virtual environment activated, you can now install the necessary libraries for finetuning GPT models. The primary libraries include:

Transformers: This library, developed by Hugging Face, provides pretrained models and tools for finetuning.

Torch: PyTorch is a deep learning framework that is commonly used for training neural networks, including GPT models.

Datasets: This library is useful for loading and preprocessing datasets.

Other Dependencies: You may need additional libraries such as `pandas`, `numpy`, and `scikitlearn` for data manipulation and evaluation.

To install these libraries, run the following command:
```

```bash
pip install torch transformers datasets pandas numpy scikitlearn
```

4. Verify Installation:

After installing the libraries, verify that everything is working correctly by checking the versions of the key libraries:

```python
import torch
import transformers
import datasets
print("Torch version:", torch.__version__)
print("Transformers version:", transformers.__version__)
print("Datasets version:", datasets.__version__)
```

5. Setting Up GPU Support (Optional):

If you have access to a GPU (Graphics Processing Unit), you can significantly speed up the finetuning process. Ensure that you have installed the appropriate CUDA and cuDNN libraries for your GPU. If you're using PyTorch, you can install the GPU version with:

DATA COLLECTION AND PREPARATION

Best Practices for Gathering and Formatting Training Data

When it comes to finetuning GPT models, the quality and relevance of your training data can significantly impact the performance and effectiveness of the model. Here are some best practices for collecting and formatting training data:

1. Define Your Objective:

Before gathering data, clarify the specific tasks you want the finetuned model to perform. Whether it's generating creative writing, answering questions, or performing text classification, understanding your objectives will guide your data collection process.

2. Identify Relevant Data Sources:

Seek out diverse and reliable data sources that align with your objectives. This could include:

Public Datasets: Utilize existing datasets available in repositories like Kaggle, Hugging Face Datasets, or the UCI Machine Learning Repository. These datasets often come preprocessed and labeled.

Web Scraping: For domainspecific applications, consider web scraping relevant websites using tools like Beautiful Soup or Scrapy. Be sure to respect the website's terms of service and legal considerations when scraping.

APIs: Leverage APIs from platforms like Twitter, Reddit, or news websites to gather realtime data or domainspecific text.

3. Data Quantity:

The amount of data required can vary depending on the task. Generally, a larger dataset can lead to better model performance, as long as the data is relevant and high quality. Aim for thousands of samples for effective finetuning, but focus on quality over quantity—having a wellcurated dataset can be more beneficial than a massive collection of irrelevant text.

4. Data Formatting:

Properly format the data to ensure it is compatible with the model. For GPT models, the text should be cleaned and structured appropriately. Common formatting considerations include:

Tokenization: Use the tokenizer provided by the Hugging Face Transformers library to convert text into tokens that the model can understand.

Input Structure: Depending on the task, structure your input data correctly. For example, if finetuning for a questionanswering task, your data might need to be formatted as pairs of questions and corresponding answers.

Text Normalization: Clean the text by removing irrelevant characters, correcting spelling errors, and ensuring consistent casing (e.g., all lowercase).

5. Splitting the Dataset:

Divide your dataset into three parts: training, validation, and testing sets. A common split might allocate 70% of the data for training, 15% for validation, and 15% for testing. This division allows you to train the model on one subset while evaluating its performance on unseen data, ensuring that the model generalizes well.

IMPORTANCE OF DATA QUALITY AND DIVERSITY IN FINETUNING

1. Data Quality:

Highquality data is crucial for training effective models. Lowquality data, which may include errors, irrelevant information, or noise, can lead to poor model performance and unexpected outputs. Consider the following aspects of data quality:

Accuracy: Ensure that the data accurately represents the concepts you wish to model. This includes correct information, relevant context, and appropriate language use.

Relevance: The data should be relevant to the specific task. For instance, if you're finetuning a model for medical applications, the training data should consist of medical texts, articles, and clinical notes, rather than general content.

Consistency: The data should maintain a consistent format, style, and language to help the model learn effectively. Inconsistent formatting can confuse the model and lead to mixed outputs.

2. Data Diversity:

Incorporating a diverse dataset is vital to ensure that the finetuned model performs well across various contexts and inputs. Diversity can enhance the model's ability to generalize and adapt to different scenarios. Consider these factors regarding data diversity:

Representation of Different Perspectives: A diverse dataset should include various viewpoints, dialects, and cultural references to avoid bias. For example, if finetuning a model for customer service, the data should encompass interactions from diverse demographics.

Variety of Content Types: Incorporate various content types and styles, such as articles, social media posts, technical documents, and conversational data. This variety helps the model understand different writing styles and contexts.

Handling Edge Cases: By including rare or edge cases in your dataset, you can improve the model's robustness. For instance, if finetuning for sentiment analysis, ensure the dataset includes examples of both positive and negative sentiments across different contexts.

3. Monitoring and Evaluation:

After collecting and preparing your dataset, it's essential to monitor the performance of your finetuned model using the validation and testing sets. Regularly evaluate the model's outputs and performance metrics to identify any issues related to data quality or representation. If the model exhibits biases or inaccuracies, consider revisiting your dataset to improve its quality and diversity.

In summary, the success of finetuning GPT models heavily relies on gathering and preparing highquality, relevant, and diverse training data. By following best practices in data collection and emphasizing the importance of data quality and diversity, you can enhance the model's performance and applicability in realworld scenarios. With a solid dataset in hand, you will be wellequipped to proceed with the finetuning process and unlock the full potential of GPT models for your specific tasks.Required Libraries and Dependencies

Here's a closer look at the essential libraries you'll need for finetuning GPT models, along with their roles:

1. Transformers:

Developed by Hugging Face, this library provides stateoftheart pretrained models and tokenizers for various NLP tasks. It includes implementations of GPT2, GPT3, and other transformer models, making it easy to load and finetune these architectures.

2. Torch (PyTorch):

PyTorch is a popular deep learning framework that provides the flexibility needed for building and training complex neural networks. It supports dynamic computation graphs, which can be particularly useful when experimenting with different model architectures and training techniques.

3. Datasets:

This library offers tools to easily load and preprocess datasets for NLP tasks. It provides access to a variety of datasets and simplifies the process of managing training and evaluation data, making it easier to focus on model finetuning.

4. Pandas:

A powerful data manipulation library, Pandas is widely used for handling structured data. It allows you to easily read, write, and manipulate datasets, making it ideal for preprocessing data before finetuning.

5. NumPy:

NumPy is essential for numerical computations and is often used for handling arrays and matrices. It provides a solid foundation for data manipulation and is commonly used alongside Pandas.

6. ScikitLearn:

This library is useful for evaluating model performance. It provides tools for splitting datasets, calculating metrics, and performing various machine learning tasks that may be relevant during the finetuning process.

By following these steps and utilizing the specified libraries, you'll create a robust environment for finetuning GPT models in

Python. This setup will empower you to leverage the full capabilities of GPT, allowing you to customize it effectively for your specific tasks and applications. With the groundwork laid, you're ready to dive into the practical aspects of finetuning and customizing GPT models to meet your specific needs.

INITIALIZING AND CONFIGURING THE GPT MODEL

Loading Pretrained GPT Models in Python

To finetune a GPT model effectively, you first need to load a pretrained version of the model using the Hugging Face Transformers library. This library provides a straightforward way to access a wide range of pretrained models, including various versions of GPT. Here's how to load a pretrained GPT model in Python:

1. Import Required Libraries:

Start by importing the necessary libraries. You will need the `transformers` library to access the GPT models and `torch` for managing PyTorch tensors.

```python
```

```python
import torch

from transformers import GPT2LMHeadModel, GPT2Tokenizer
```

2. Loading the Tokenizer:

The tokenizer converts text into a format that the model can process. For GPT2, you can load the pretrained tokenizer as follows:

```python
tokenizer = GPT2Tokenizer.from_pretrained('gpt2')
```

3. Loading the Pretrained Model:

Load the pretrained GPT2 model using the `from_pretrained` method. This method fetches the model weights and configuration from the Hugging Face model hub.

```python
model = GPT2LMHeadModel.from_pretrained('gpt2')
```

```
```

4. Setting the Model to Evaluation Mode:

Before finetuning, it's advisable to set the model to evaluation mode. This is done to deactivate layers like dropout, which are used during training but should not affect inference or validation.

```python
model.eval()
```

5. Checking for GPU Availability (Optional):

If you have a GPU available, loading the model onto the GPU will significantly speed up the training process. You can check for GPU availability and move the model and tokenizer to the GPU as follows:

```python
device = torch.device("cuda" if torch.cuda.is_available() else "cpu")

model.to(device)
```

```
```

By following these steps, you will successfully load a pretrained GPT model into your Python environment, setting the stage for the finetuning process.

CONFIGURATION SETTINGS FOR OPTIMAL PERFORMANCE

Finetuning a GPT model requires configuring various settings to achieve optimal performance tailored to your specific tasks. The configuration can influence training speed, model performance, and the quality of generated outputs. Here are some critical configuration settings to consider:

1. Model Configuration:

The `GPT2Config` class allows you to customize the model architecture. You can specify parameters such as the number of layers, hidden size, and attention heads. For example:

```python
from transformers import GPT2Config

config = GPT2Config.from_pretrained('gpt2')
```

```
config.num_hidden_layers = 12   Default for GPT2

config.hidden_size = 768         Default for GPT2

config.num_attention_heads = 12   Default for GPT2
```

2. Learning Rate:

The learning rate is one of the most critical hyperparameters affecting the finetuning process. A lower learning rate can help the model learn more effectively, while a higher rate can speed up training but may risk overshooting optimal weights. Start with a learning rate around `5e5` to `2e5` for finetuning tasks:

```python
from transformers import AdamW

learning_rate = 5e5

optimizer = AdamW(model.parameters(), lr=learning_rate)
```

3. Batch Size:

The batch size determines how many samples are processed before the model's internal parameters are updated. A larger batch size can lead to faster training but requires more GPU memory. A common starting point is a batch size of 8 or 16. You can adjust it based on your hardware capabilities:

```python
batch_size = 8   Adjust based on your GPU memory
```

4. Number of Epochs:

The number of epochs refers to how many times the training process iterates over the entire dataset. Start with 3 to 5 epochs for finetuning, and monitor the model's performance on the validation set to avoid overfitting:

```python
num_epochs = 3   Adjust based on model performance
```

5. Gradient Accumulation:

If you're limited by GPU memory and cannot increase the batch size, consider using gradient accumulation. This technique allows you to simulate larger batch sizes by accumulating gradients over several steps before performing an optimization step:

```python
accumulation_steps = 4   Accumulate gradients over 4 steps
```

6. Checkpointing:

Implementing checkpointing saves the model's weights at regular intervals, allowing you to restore the model if the training process is interrupted. You can set up checkpointing to save the model after every epoch or based on validation performance:

```python
from transformers import Trainer, TrainingArguments
training_args = TrainingArguments(
    output_dir='./results',
```

```
    evaluation_strategy="epoch",

    save_strategy="epoch",

    save_total_limit=2,

)
```
```

## 7. Early Stopping:

Early stopping is a technique that halts training when the model's performance on the validation set stops improving. This can help prevent overfitting and save computational resources. You can implement early stopping by monitoring validation loss and setting a patience parameter:

```python

patience = 2    Number of epochs to wait before stopping if no improvement

```

8. Mixed Precision Training (Optional):
```

If your hardware supports it, consider using mixed precision training to speed up the training process while using less memory. This technique involves using both 16bit and 32bit floatingpoint types. The `transformers` library supports mixed precision with `torch.cuda.amp`:

```python
from torch.cuda.amp import GradScaler, autocast
scaler = GradScaler()
```

By initializing and configuring the GPT model with these considerations, you set the foundation for a successful finetuning process. Proper configuration ensures that the model can learn effectively from your dataset, enabling it to generate highquality outputs that meet your specific needs. With the model loaded and configured, you're ready to proceed with the finetuning process, adapting the GPT architecture to excel in your chosen applications.

Chapter 3

Techniques for FineTuning GPT Models

UNDERSTANDING TRANSFER LEARNING IN GPT

Introduction to Transfer Learning

Transfer learning is a powerful technique in machine learning and deep learning that allows models trained on one task to be adapted and reused for another task. In the context of GPT (Generative Pretrained Transformer) models, transfer learning involves taking a pretrained model that has been trained on a large corpus of text data and finetuning it on a smaller, taskspecific dataset. This approach not only accelerates the training process but also improves the model's performance on the target task due to the knowledge the model has already acquired.

THE PRETRAINING PHASE

1. Pretraining GPT Models:

The first step in transfer learning with GPT models is pretraining. During this phase, the model is trained on vast amounts of unlabeled text data to learn the underlying structure of the language. The objective is typically to predict the next word in a sentence given the previous words (also known as language modeling). This process allows the model to capture various aspects of language, such as grammar, syntax, semantics, and even some world knowledge.

GPT models utilize a transformer architecture, which leverages selfattention mechanisms to process text efficiently. By attending to different parts of the input text, the model learns contextual relationships between words, making it highly effective at generating coherent and contextually relevant text.

2. Benefits of Pretraining:

The advantage of pretraining is that it enables the model to develop a robust understanding of language before it is finetuned for specific tasks. Because the model has already seen a diverse range of text during pretraining, it can generalize better when exposed to new data in finetuning.

Additionally, pretraining on large datasets allows the model to learn intricate patterns in language, which may be difficult to capture if the model were trained solely on a smaller, taskspecific dataset. This results in improved performance in various natural language processing (NLP) tasks, such as text classification, question answering, and sentiment analysis.

THE FINETUNING PHASE

1. FineTuning Process:

After pretraining, the GPT model is finetuned on a smaller dataset that is specific to the target task. This involves adjusting the model's weights to optimize its performance for the desired application. Finetuning typically requires fewer training epochs than pretraining due to the foundational knowledge the model has already acquired.

The finetuning process can be tailored to suit various NLP tasks. For example, if the goal is to generate creative writing, the finetuning dataset might consist of literary texts, while for a questionanswering application, the dataset would include questionanswer pairs.

2. Advantages of FineTuning:

Finetuning allows developers to leverage the power of large pretrained models without the need for extensive computational resources or large labeled datasets. Since the model has already learned useful language representations, finetuning can often be accomplished with relatively small datasets, making it feasible for applications where data is scarce.

This approach also reduces training time, as the model begins with weights that are already close to an optimal solution. Consequently, finetuning can lead to faster convergence and better performance compared to training a model from scratch.

KEY CONCEPTS IN TRANSFER LEARNING WITH GPT

1. Domain Adaptation:

Transfer learning is particularly effective when adapting models to new domains. For instance, a GPT model pretrained on general text can be finetuned on medical literature to improve its ability to generate and understand healthcarerelated content. This process allows the model to adapt its language understanding to the specific terminologies and styles relevant to the new domain.

2. TaskSpecific Customization:

Different tasks may require different model behaviors, and finetuning allows for this customization. By providing the model with a specific dataset related to the desired task, you guide the model in adjusting its outputs accordingly. For example, if finetuning for a customer service chatbot, you would use transcripts of customer interactions to shape the model's responses.

3. Transfer of Knowledge:

The core idea of transfer learning is the transfer of knowledge from one domain or task to another. In GPT models, this transfer occurs during finetuning, where the knowledge acquired during pretraining is adapted to the specifics of the new task. This knowledge transfer can lead to improved performance on tasks where data is limited or hard to obtain.

BEST PRACTICES FOR FINETUNING GPT MODELS

1. Selecting an Appropriate Dataset:

When finetuning, it is crucial to select a dataset that closely aligns with the intended application. The dataset should be relevant, diverse, and representative of the types of text the model will encounter in realworld use. Higher quality datasets lead to better model performance.

2. Monitoring Performance:

During the finetuning process, continuously monitor the model's performance using validation datasets. Track metrics such as loss, accuracy, and perplexity to ensure the model is learning effectively. Early stopping can also be employed to halt training when performance plateaus, preventing overfitting.

3. Experimentation with Hyperparameters:

Experiment with different hyperparameters, including learning rates, batch sizes, and epoch counts. Finetuning hyperparameters can significantly influence the model's ability to learn effectively from the dataset.

4. Utilizing Pretrained Checkpoints:

Depending on the task, you may want to use different versions of pretrained GPT models (e.g., GPT2, GPT3, or GPT4). Evaluate various checkpoints to find the one that works best for your specific finetuning goals.

5. Regularization Techniques:

Incorporate regularization techniques such as dropout or weight decay to prevent overfitting, particularly when working with smaller datasets. Regularization helps ensure that the model generalizes well to unseen data.

Understanding transfer learning is crucial for effectively finetuning GPT models. By leveraging the knowledge gained during pretraining and applying it to specific tasks through finetuning, developers can create powerful NLP applications with significantly less data and computational resources. Transfer learning not only enhances the model's performance but also allows for quick adaptation to diverse applications across various domains, making it a cornerstone of modern NLP techniques. As you continue your journey in finetuning GPT models, embrace the principles of transfer learning to unlock the full potential of these powerful language models.

FINETUNING WITH CUSTOM DATASETS

StepbyStep Guide to FineTuning GPT with a Custom Dataset

Finetuning a GPT model with a custom dataset involves several systematic steps, from data preparation to training and evaluation. This process allows you to tailor the model's outputs to meet specific requirements, ensuring that it generates relevant and highquality text. Here's a detailed guide on how to effectively finetune GPT with a custom dataset:

1. Define Your Objectives:

Before starting the finetuning process, clearly define the objectives of your project. Identify the specific task (e.g., text generation, summarization, question answering) and the intended use cases for the finetuned model. Understanding your goals will help shape the data preparation and training process.

2. Collect and Prepare the Dataset:

Gather a custom dataset that aligns with your defined objectives. Depending on your task, this could include:

Text documents, articles, or transcripts for text generation or summarization.

Questionanswer pairs for a chatbot or QA system.

Domainspecific texts (e.g., medical, legal) for applications in specialized fields.

Data Cleaning:

Clean and preprocess the dataset to ensure it is in a usable format. This may involve:

Removing irrelevant information (headers, footers, etc.).

Correcting grammatical errors and typos.

Ensuring consistent formatting and style.

Tokenization:

Use the appropriate tokenizer for the GPT model you are finetuning (e.g., `GPT2Tokenizer` from the Hugging Face Transformers library). Tokenization converts raw text into tokens that the model can process.

```python
from transformers import GPT2Tokenizer
tokenizer = GPT2Tokenizer.from_pretrained('gpt2')
```

```
tokenized_data = tokenizer.batch_encode_plus(

    your_dataset,

    truncation=True,

    padding=True,

    return_tensors='pt'

)
```
```

3. Split the Dataset:

Divide your dataset into training, validation, and test sets. A common split is 80% training, 10% validation, and 10% testing. The training set is used to finetune the model, the validation set is used to monitor performance and adjust hyperparameters, and the test set is used to evaluate the final model.

4. Configure the Training Environment:

Set up your Python environment with the necessary libraries. Ensure you have the Hugging Face Transformers library installed, along with other dependencies like PyTorch or TensorFlow.
```

```bash
pip install transformers torch
```

5. Load the Pretrained GPT Model:

Load the pretrained GPT model you want to finetune. For example, you can use the GPT2 model from the Hugging Face model hub.

```python
from transformers import GPT2LMHeadModel


model = GPT2LMHeadModel.from_pretrained('gpt2')
model.train()   Set the model to training mode
```

6. Set Training Hyperparameters:

Define your training hyperparameters, such as:

Learning Rate: A common starting point is between `1e5` and `5e5`. You may need to experiment to find the optimal learning rate.

Batch Size: Depending on your GPU memory, start with a batch size of 8 or 16.

Number of Epochs: Begin with 3 to 5 epochs and adjust based on validation performance.

```python
from transformers import AdamW

learning_rate = 5e5

batch_size = 8

num_epochs = 3

optimizer = AdamW(model.parameters(), lr=learning_rate)
```

7. Create a DataLoader:

Use a DataLoader to efficiently load your training and validation data in batches during training. The DataLoader handles shuffling and batching of your dataset.

```python
from torch.utils.data import DataLoader, Dataset

class CustomDataset(Dataset):
    def __init__(self, tokenized_data):
        self.data = tokenized_data

    def __len__(self):
        return len(self.data['input_ids'])

    def __getitem__(self, idx):
        return {
            'input_ids': self.data['input_ids'][idx],
            'attention_mask': self.data['attention_mask'][idx]
        }

train_dataset = CustomDataset(tokenized_data)
```

```python
    train_loader                =               DataLoader(train_dataset,
batch_size=batch_size, shuffle=True)
```

8. FineTuning the Model:

Start the finetuning process by iterating through the training data. For each epoch, pass the training data through the model, compute the loss, and update the model weights using backpropagation.

```python
from transformers import Trainer, TrainingArguments

training_args = TrainingArguments(
    output_dir='./results',
    num_train_epochs=num_epochs,
    per_device_train_batch_size=batch_size,
    evaluation_strategy='epoch',
    save_strategy='epoch',
```

```
    learning_rate=learning_rate,

)

trainer = Trainer(

    model=model,

    args=training_args,

    train_dataset=train_dataset,

    eval_dataset=validation_dataset,

)


    trainer.train()
```
```

9. Monitoring and Adjusting Learning Rates and Other Hyperparameters:

During training, it's essential to monitor the model's performance using the validation set. This can be done by tracking metrics such as loss and perplexity.
```

Learning Rate Scheduling: Consider implementing a learning rate scheduler to adjust the learning rate dynamically during training. For example, you might start with a higher learning rate and gradually decrease it. The Hugging Face library supports various scheduling strategies.

```python
from transformers import get_linear_schedule_with_warmup

total_steps = len(train_loader) * num_epochs

scheduler = get_linear_schedule_with_warmup(
    optimizer,
    num_warmup_steps=0,
    num_training_steps=total_steps
)

for epoch in range(num_epochs):
    for batch in train_loader:
        optimizer.zero_grad()
```

```
    outputs           =           model(batch['input_ids'],
attention_mask=batch['attention_mask'])

    loss = outputs.loss

    loss.backward()

    optimizer.step()

    scheduler.step()   Update the learning rate
```

Early Stopping: Implement early stopping to halt training if validation performance does not improve after a certain number of epochs (patience). This helps to prevent overfitting.

```python
 Pseudocode for early stopping

best_loss = float('inf')

patience = 3

patience_counter = 0

for epoch in range(num_epochs):
```

```
    Training loop...

    validation_loss = evaluate(model, validation_loader)

    if validation_loss < best_loss:

        best_loss = validation_loss

        patience_counter = 0

         Save the best model

    else:

        patience_counter += 1

        if patience_counter >= patience:

            print("Early stopping triggered")

            break
```
```

10. Evaluate the Model:

After finetuning, evaluate the model on the test dataset to assess its performance. Use metrics relevant to your task, such as accuracy, F1 score, or BLEU score for text generation tasks. This
```

evaluation will give you insights into how well the model performs on unseen data.

```python
test_loss = evaluate(model, test_loader)

print(f'Test Loss: {test_loss}')
```

11. Saving the FineTuned Model:

Once finetuning is complete and you are satisfied with the model's performance, save the finetuned model for future use. The Hugging Face library allows you to easily save and load models.

```python
model.save_pretrained('./fine_tuned_model')

tokenizer.save_pretrained('./fine_tuned_model')
```

12. Deployment and Inference:

The final step is to deploy the finetuned model for inference. You can load the model from the saved directory and use it to generate predictions or text based on new inputs.

```python
from transformers import pipeline

fine_tuned_model = GPT2LMHeadModel.from_pretrained('./fine_tuned_model')

fine_tuned_tokenizer = GPT2Tokenizer.from_pretrained('./fine_tuned_model')

text_generator = pipeline('textgeneration', model=fine_tuned_model, tokenizer=fine_tuned_tokenizer)

generated_text = text_generator("Your prompt here", max_length=100)

print(generated_text)
```

Finetuning GPT models with custom datasets is a systematic and iterative process that allows developers to leverage pretrained models for specific applications. By following the stepbystep guide outlined above, you can effectively customize GPT to suit your needs, improving its performance on particular tasks while capitalizing on the extensive knowledge acquired during pretraining. Monitoring and adjusting hyperparameters, especially learning rates, play a crucial role in this process, ensuring that the model learns efficiently and generalizes well to unseen data. With careful data preparation and thorough evaluation, finetuning can unlock the full potential of GPT models, enabling the development of powerful and effective natural language processing applications.

EVALUATING AND IMPROVING MODEL PERFORMANCE

Metrics for Evaluating the Effectiveness of FineTuning

Evaluating the performance of finetuned GPT models is crucial to ensure they meet the desired objectives and perform well on specific tasks. Here are some key metrics and methods to assess the effectiveness of finetuning:

1. Loss Function:

The loss function quantifies how well the model's predictions align with the actual outcomes. For language models, the common loss function used is crossentropy loss, which measures the difference between the predicted probability distribution and the true distribution of the next token.

Monitoring loss during training helps track how well the model learns. A decreasing loss indicates that the model is improving. However, it's essential to also evaluate loss on a validation set to avoid overfitting.

```python
Example of tracking loss during training

training_loss = []

validation_loss = []

for epoch in range(num_epochs):

    epoch_loss = 0

    for batch in train_loader:

        Forward pass, loss computation, and backpropagation
```

```
    ...

    epoch_loss += loss.item()

  training_loss.append(epoch_loss / len(train_loader))

  val_loss = evaluate(model, validation_loader)

  validation_loss.append(val_loss)
```

2. Perplexity:

Perplexity is a common metric used in language modeling to evaluate how well a probability distribution predicts a sample. It is calculated as the exponentiation of the average negative loglikelihood of a sequence. Lower perplexity indicates better performance.

Perplexity can be useful for comparing models or configurations, especially during hyperparameter tuning.

```python
from math import exp

def calculate_perplexity(loss):
```

```python
    return exp(loss)

val_perplexity = calculate_perplexity(val_loss)

print(f'Validation Perplexity: {val_perplexity}')
```

3. BLEU Score:

The BLEU (Bilingual Evaluation Understudy) score is commonly used to evaluate the quality of generated text by comparing it to reference texts. It's particularly useful in tasks like text generation and machine translation.

BLEU scores range from 0 to 1, where a higher score indicates a better match with the reference texts.

```python
from nltk.translate.bleu_score import sentence_bleu

reference = [["the", "cat", "is", "on", "the", "mat"]]

candidate = ["the", "cat", "is", "on", "the", "mat"]

bleu_score = sentence_bleu(reference, candidate)
```

```
print(f'BLEU Score: {bleu_score}')
```

4. ROUGE Score:

ROUGE (RecallOriented Understudy for Gisting Evaluation) is another metric commonly used for evaluating generated summaries. It compares the overlap of ngrams between generated and reference summaries.

ROUGE scores provide a way to measure recall, precision, and F1 scores, making them useful for summarization tasks.

```python
from rouge import Rouge

rouge = Rouge()

scores = rouge.get_scores(generated_summary, reference_summary)

print(f'ROUGE Scores: {scores}')
```

5. Accuracy:

For specific tasks such as classification or question answering, accuracy can be a straightforward metric to evaluate the model's performance. It measures the proportion of correct predictions among the total predictions made.

This is particularly relevant for finetuning models on datasets with labeled examples.

TECHNIQUES FOR ITERATIVE IMPROVEMENT AND ERROR ANALYSIS

Improving model performance is an ongoing process that involves careful analysis and adjustments. Here are some techniques to iteratively enhance the performance of finetuned GPT models:

1. Error Analysis:

After evaluating the model, conduct a thorough error analysis to identify common patterns in the errors. This can involve:

Reviewing incorrect outputs to understand why the model failed.

Categorizing errors (e.g., context misunderstanding, factual inaccuracies) to identify specific areas for improvement.

For instance, if the model frequently generates irrelevant text, it may be beneficial to refine the training data or adjust the model's architecture.

2. Data Augmentation:

Enhance the training dataset by using data augmentation techniques. This can include:

Synonym replacement: Replacing words with synonyms to diversify the training data.

Backtranslation: Translating text to another language and back to increase diversity and reduce biases.

Augmenting the dataset can help improve model robustness and generalization.

3. Hyperparameter Tuning:

Experiment with different hyperparameters, such as learning rates, batch sizes, and the number of epochs. Utilizing techniques like grid search or random search can help identify optimal configurations.

Consider using a learning rate scheduler to adjust the learning rate dynamically during training. This can help stabilize training and improve convergence.

4. Regularization Techniques:

Apply regularization techniques such as dropout or weight decay to mitigate overfitting. These methods can help improve the model's generalization to unseen data.

```python
from transformers import GPT2LMHeadModel, GPT2Config

config = GPT2Config.from_pretrained('gpt2', dropout=0.1)
Set dropout rate

model = GPT2LMHeadModel(config)
```

5. Transfer Learning from Other Tasks:

If your dataset is limited, consider leveraging transfer learning from related tasks. Finetuning on a larger, related dataset can help the model learn better representations before applying it to your specific task.

For example, if finetuning a GPT model for customer support, consider first finetuning on a more extensive dataset related to general dialogue or customer interactions.

6. Continuous Learning:

Implement a continuous learning framework where the model is periodically updated with new data. As new data becomes available, retrain the model to ensure it stays relevant and maintains high performance.

This can also involve feedback loops where user interactions provide additional data for retraining.

7. Ensemble Methods:

Consider using ensemble methods by combining multiple models to improve overall performance. This can involve averaging predictions from different models or using a voting mechanism to make decisions.

Ensembles can help mitigate individual model biases and improve robustness.

8. User Feedback:

Collect user feedback on model outputs to identify areas for improvement. This can involve surveys or direct input from users who interact with the model.

User insights can provide valuable information on performance and highlight specific aspects of the model that may require adjustments.

By systematically evaluating model performance using appropriate metrics and employing iterative improvement techniques, developers can enhance the quality and effectiveness of finetuned GPT models. This ongoing process not only improves the model's capabilities but also ensures it aligns with user needs and expectations, resulting in more reliable and contextually relevant outputs.

Chapter 4

Advanced Customization Techniques

TOKENIZATION AND PREPROCESSING STRATEGIES

Custom Tokenization Techniques for DomainSpecific Language

Tokenization is a crucial step in the preprocessing of text data for training and finetuning GPT models. It involves breaking down the text into smaller units, typically words or subwords, which the model can understand. For domainspecific applications, customizing the tokenization process can significantly enhance the model's performance by better capturing the nuances and vocabulary specific to the domain. Here are some strategies for effective tokenization and preprocessing:

1. Understanding Tokenization:

Tokenization involves segmenting text into tokens, which can be words, subwords, or characters. For example, the sentence "Artificial Intelligence is fascinating" might be tokenized into ["Artificial", "Intelligence", "is", "fascinating"].

GPT models, particularly those based on the Transformer architecture, often use subword tokenization techniques such as Byte Pair Encoding (BPE) or WordPiece. These methods allow the model to handle rare words by breaking them down into smaller, more frequent components.

2. DomainSpecific Vocabulary:

In many specialized fields (e.g., medicine, law, finance), certain terms and acronyms may not be wellrepresented in general language models. To address this, it may be necessary to create a custom vocabulary that includes domainspecific terms.

Start by compiling a list of frequently used terms and phrases in your specific domain. This can be done through text analysis of relevant documents, articles, and literature.

Update the tokenizer's vocabulary with these terms to ensure that the model recognizes and correctly handles them during training and inference.

3. Custom Tokenizers:

Use custom tokenization methods that are tailored to the structure of domainspecific text. For instance, if dealing with scientific texts, you may want to preserve certain multiword expressions (e.g., "machine learning" or "natural language processing") as single tokens.

Implementing custom tokenizers can involve modifying existing libraries like Hugging Face's `tokenizers` or building a new tokenizer from scratch using regular expressions or rulebased approaches.

4. Handling Special Characters and Formats:

Different domains often have unique formats and special characters (e.g., chemical formulas, programming code snippets). Custom tokenization should account for these to maintain the integrity of the data.

For example, in the chemical domain, it's essential to ensure that formulas like H2O or C6H12O6 are preserved as single tokens. Similarly, in programming, syntax and code structures must be accurately represented.

```python
import re

def custom_tokenizer(text):

    Preserve chemical formulas as tokens

    text = re.sub(r'\bH\dO\b', 'H2O', text)    Example regex for H2O

    text = re.sub(r'\bC\dH\dO\d\b', 'C6H12O6', text)    Example for glucose

    tokens = text.split()    Simple whitespace tokenization

    return tokens

```

5. Subword Tokenization:

Consider implementing subword tokenization techniques that allow the model to break down unknown words into smaller, recognizable parts. This is particularly useful for technical jargon or newly coined terms that may not exist in standard vocabularies.

BPE and WordPiece can be implemented using libraries like Hugging Face's `tokenizers` package, which provides flexible methods for creating and training tokenizers based on your data.

```python
from tokenizers import ByteLevelBPETokenizer

Initialize a tokenizer

tokenizer = ByteLevelBPETokenizer()

Train the tokenizer on domainspecific corpus

tokenizer.train_from_file('domain_specific_corpus.txt')

Encode text

tokens = tokenizer.encode("This is a domainspecific sentence.")
```

6. Text Normalization:

Implement text normalization techniques to preprocess the input data effectively. This may include converting text to lowercase, removing punctuation, or standardizing certain terms (e.g., expanding contractions).

Additionally, consider stemming or lemmatization to reduce words to their base forms, which can help the model generalize better across different contexts.

```python
from nltk.stem import WordNetLemmatizer

import string

lemmatizer = WordNetLemmatizer()

def normalize_text(text):

    Lowercase and remove punctuation

    text = text.lower().translate(str.maketrans('', '', string.punctuation))

    Lemmatize

    tokens = text.split()
```

```
tokens = [lemmatizer.lemmatize(token) for token in tokens]

return tokens
```

```

7. Training a Custom Tokenizer:

Once you have gathered domainspecific data and created a custom vocabulary, you can train a tokenizer specifically for your needs. This involves analyzing the text corpus and adapting the tokenization process to maximize performance.

The training process typically involves feeding the corpus into a tokenizer model that learns the best way to segment the text into meaningful tokens, balancing vocabulary size and token frequency.

8. Evaluation of Tokenization:

After implementing a custom tokenizer, it's essential to evaluate its effectiveness. Test the tokenizer on various samples from your domain to ensure it accurately captures relevant terminology and handles edge cases appropriately.
```

Metrics such as tokenization speed, vocabulary size, and the proportion of unrecognized tokens can help assess the performance of your tokenizer.

By employing these custom tokenization and preprocessing strategies, developers can significantly enhance the ability of GPT models to understand and generate text that is relevant to specific domains. This tailored approach not only improves model accuracy but also ensures that it can effectively handle the complexities and nuances associated with specialized language, ultimately leading to more effective applications of GPT technology.

STRATEGIES FOR HANDLING OUTOFVOCABULARY WORDS AND RARE TOKENS

Handling outofvocabulary (OOV) words and rare tokens is a critical challenge in natural language processing (NLP), particularly when finetuning models like GPT. Outofvocabulary words are those not present in the model's vocabulary, while rare tokens may occur infrequently in the training data, making them less wellrepresented in the model's learned parameters. Here are several strategies to effectively address these challenges:

1. Subword Tokenization:

Byte Pair Encoding (BPE): This technique helps mitigate the issue of OOV words by breaking down words into subword units. By using a corpus of text to iteratively merge the most frequently occurring pairs of characters or subwords, BPE allows the tokenizer to create a vocabulary that includes parts of words, thus facilitating better handling of rare or unseen terms.

WordPiece: Similar to BPE, WordPiece tokenization builds a vocabulary based on subwords, but it focuses on maximizing the likelihood of the training data given the vocabulary. This approach is particularly effective in retaining meaning and context for OOV words.

For example, the word "unhappiness" could be tokenized into ["un", "happi", "ness"], allowing the model to still infer meaning from the known subwords.

2. CharacterLevel Tokenization:

In some cases, using a characterlevel tokenizer can help ensure that all words, regardless of their frequency or presence in the vocabulary, are represented. Characterlevel tokenization breaks down all words into individual characters, enabling the model to reconstruct any OOV words.

Although this approach can handle all words, it may lead to longer sequences, potentially increasing computational costs and reducing the model's ability to learn longrange dependencies. Nevertheless, it can be beneficial in specific applications, such as those involving languages with rich morphology or when dealing with technical jargon.

3. Use of Special Tokens:

Introduce special tokens to represent unknown words or rare tokens. For instance, many tokenization frameworks utilize an "[UNK]" (unknown) token for OOV words. When encountering an OOV word during preprocessing, it can be replaced with the "[UNK]" token, allowing the model to maintain a fixed vocabulary size.

However, care should be taken with this strategy, as it may lead to the loss of important semantic information. To mitigate this, you can create additional tokens to capture specific outofvocabulary terms relevant to your domain.

4. Data Augmentation:

Data augmentation techniques can help create more diverse training examples, increasing the likelihood that rare tokens will appear during training. This can include synonym replacement, paraphrasing, and backtranslation.

For example, if your dataset includes the rare term "neuroplasticity," you could augment the dataset by generating synonyms or related phrases like "brain adaptability" or "neural flexibility" to help the model better recognize and understand the concept.

5. Dynamic Vocabulary Updates:

Implement a dynamic vocabulary that can be updated based on the training data. This approach involves periodically analyzing the training corpus and adjusting the vocabulary to include new words that are encountered frequently.

This strategy allows for the ongoing adaptation of the model to new terminology without requiring a complete retraining of the vocabulary. Techniques like online learning can help facilitate this process.

6. Fallback Mechanisms:

Implement fallback mechanisms that allow the model to leverage context when encountering OOV words. For instance, if a word is not recognized, the model can look at the surrounding context (the preceding and following words) to infer meaning based on the context in which the OOV word appears.

This can involve additional layers of contextaware processing that help the model make educated guesses about the meaning of OOV words based on semantic similarity to known words.

7. DomainSpecific Preprocessing:

When working within a specific domain, create a list of frequently used terms and abbreviations specific to that domain. This list can be utilized to ensure that these terms are included in the vocabulary.

Consider using domainspecific corpora to train the tokenizer, which can help reduce the likelihood of encountering OOV words by ensuring that the vocabulary is representative of the specific language and terminology used in that field.

8. Word Clustering:

Utilize word clustering techniques to group similar words together. This approach involves creating clusters of words that share similar meanings or contexts, which can be helpful when an OOV word is encountered. By clustering words based on their contextual usage, the model can make inferences about OOV words based on their proximity to known words in the same cluster.

Techniques like Word2Vec or GloVe can be useful for generating word embeddings that capture semantic similarities between words, allowing for better handling of OOV words.

9. Training with Diverse Data:

Ensure that the training data is diverse and representative of the language that the model will encounter during deployment. The more varied the data, the better the chances of including rare tokens and OOV words.

Collecting data from multiple sources, including social media, technical articles, and domainspecific literature, can help enrich the vocabulary and reduce the impact of OOV words.

10. PostProcessing Techniques:

Implement postprocessing techniques to handle OOV words in generated outputs. For instance, if the model generates an OOV word, a postprocessing step can analyze the context and replace it with the nearest known synonym or a more commonly used term.

This step can improve the fluency and coherence of the generated text, making it more readable and relatable to the target audience.

By employing these strategies, developers can enhance the ability of GPT models to handle outofvocabulary words and rare tokens effectively. This approach not only improves the model's performance in generating relevant and coherent text but also ensures that it can adapt to the evolving language landscape within specific domains, ultimately leading to more accurate and contextually appropriate outputs.

MODIFYING GPT ARCHITECTURES

Exploring the Potential for Architectural Modifications

Modifying the architecture of GPT models can significantly enhance their performance for specific tasks or applications. While the standard GPT architecture is powerful, customization through architectural modifications allows developers to tailor the model to better suit their needs. This section explores various strategies for modifying GPT architectures, including the introduction of custom layers, adjustments to attention mechanisms, and their overall impact on performance.

1. Understanding the Standard GPT Architecture:

The GPT architecture is based on the Transformer model, which consists of a stack of transformer blocks. Each block includes multihead selfattention layers and feedforward neural networks (FFNNs). The original GPT1, GPT2, GPT3, and GPT4 architectures have progressively increased in complexity, scale, and performance capabilities.

A typical transformer block in GPT consists of:

MultiHead SelfAttention: Allows the model to focus on different parts of the input sequence simultaneously, learning contextual relationships.

FeedForward Neural Network (FFNN): Applies nonlinear transformations to the attention outputs, enabling the model to learn complex patterns.

Layer Normalization and Residual Connections: Enhance training stability and model performance by facilitating better gradient flow.

2. Custom Layers:

Introduction of New Layers: Depending on the specific application, you may consider adding custom layers to the GPT architecture. For instance, incorporating convolutional layers can help capture local patterns in text data, improving performance in tasks such as sentiment analysis or entity recognition.

TaskSpecific Layers: For specialized tasks, such as sequence classification or token classification, additional output layers tailored to the specific task can be integrated. For example, adding a softmax layer for multiclass classification can enhance the model's ability to produce relevant outputs for tasks like sentiment classification or topic identification.

```python
import torch.nn as nn

class CustomGPTModel(nn.Module):

    def __init__(self, gpt_model):
```

```
        super(CustomGPTModel, self).__init__()

        self.gpt = gpt_model

        self.custom_layer                              =
nn.Linear(gpt_model.config.hidden_size, num_classes)

    def forward(self, input_ids):

        outputs = self.gpt(input_ids)

        logits = self.custom_layer(outputs.last_hidden_state)

        return logits
```
```

3. Attention Mechanism Modifications:

Alternative Attention Mechanisms: While the standard selfattention mechanism is effective, exploring alternative attention mechanisms can yield improvements. For instance, using sparse attention can reduce computational costs and memory usage, allowing the model to scale to longer input sequences.
```

Local vs. Global Attention: Implementing local attention can help the model focus on relevant portions of the input, which is beneficial for tasks where context is limited. Conversely, global attention can be employed when understanding the entire input context is crucial.

Hierarchical Attention: In applications like document summarization, hierarchical attention mechanisms can be useful. These mechanisms enable the model to first attend to sentences within paragraphs and then to paragraphs within documents, effectively capturing the structure of long texts.

4. Modifying the FeedForward Network (FFNN):

Custom Activation Functions: The standard FFNN in GPT typically uses the ReLU activation function. Experimenting with alternative activation functions, such as Swish or GELU, can enhance the model's expressiveness and potentially improve performance on specific tasks.

MultiLayer FeedForward Networks: Increasing the depth of the feedforward network can allow the model to learn more complex representations. However, care should be taken to balance model complexity with training stability.

5. Incorporating Memory Mechanisms:

Memory Augmentation: Adding external memory components can help the model retain information over longer contexts, improving its ability to handle tasks that require understanding lengthy documents or maintaining context over extended interactions.

Attention with Memory: Combining attention mechanisms with memory can facilitate more effective information retrieval, enabling the model to leverage both learned weights and external knowledge efficiently.

6. Utilizing Pretrained Modules:

Transfer Learning: Consider integrating pretrained modules from other architectures, such as BERT or T5, into the GPT model. These modules may offer enhanced capabilities for understanding context and semantics, which can improve overall performance.

Adapter Layers: Implement adapter layers to add new functionalities without retraining the entire model. These layers allow the GPT model to adapt to specific tasks while preserving the knowledge learned during pretraining.

7. Performance Impact and Tradeoffs:

Computational Complexity: Modifications to the architecture can increase the computational complexity and resource requirements of the model. It's essential to balance the benefits of improved performance against the costs in terms of training time and resource utilization.

Evaluation Metrics: Monitor various evaluation metrics, such as accuracy, F1 score, and computational efficiency, to assess the impact of architectural modifications. Regular evaluation during development will help identify the most effective changes for the specific task.

8. Experimentation and Iteration:

Hyperparameter Tuning: After implementing architectural modifications, engage in rigorous hyperparameter tuning to optimize the model's performance. This process may involve adjusting learning rates, batch sizes, and the number of training epochs.

Iterative Testing: Conduct iterative testing to evaluate the effectiveness of the modified architecture on a validation set.

Analyze the results and make further adjustments as needed to finetune the model for optimal performance.

9. Case Studies and RealWorld Applications:

IndustrySpecific Applications: Explore case studies where modified GPT architectures have yielded successful outcomes. For instance, customizing the model for healthcare applications may involve integrating additional layers to analyze patient records or clinical notes effectively.

DomainSpecific Performance: Analyze how modifications have improved performance in areas like sentiment analysis, customer support chatbots, and automated content generation. Sharing these case studies can provide valuable insights for others seeking to implement architectural changes.

By exploring the potential for architectural modifications in GPT models, developers can significantly enhance the model's performance on specific tasks. Custom layers, tailored attention mechanisms, and other adjustments not only allow for the finetuning of the model but also open up new possibilities for applications across various domains. Through thoughtful experimentation and iteration, these modifications can lead to more effective and efficient language processing capabilities, ultimately making GPT models more powerful tools in the NLP landscape.

INCORPORATING EXTERNAL KNOWLEDGE BASES

Enhancing GPT with External Data Sources and Knowledge Graphs

Incorporating external knowledge bases into GPT models can significantly improve their performance and ability to generate accurate, contextually relevant responses. By leveraging structured and unstructured external data sources, such as knowledge graphs, databases, and APIs, developers can enrich the information available to the model, enhancing its understanding of specific domains and providing more informed predictions. This section explores techniques for integrating additional context into model predictions through the use of external knowledge bases.

1. Understanding External Knowledge Bases:

Definition: External knowledge bases refer to structured collections of information that provide additional context, facts, and relationships about entities in various domains. Examples include knowledge graphs (like DBpedia and Google Knowledge Graph), ontologies, and domainspecific databases.

Importance: These knowledge sources can help fill gaps in the training data of GPT models, enabling them to respond accurately to queries that involve factual knowledge or domainspecific information. For example, if a user asks about the symptoms of a disease, incorporating medical knowledge from a reputable database can ensure that the response is accurate and uptodate.

2. Knowledge Graph Integration:

Definition of Knowledge Graphs: Knowledge graphs are structured representations of entities and their relationships, often visualized as a network of nodes (entities) and edges (relationships). They facilitate better understanding and inference of connections between concepts.

Enhancement of GPT Models: Integrating a knowledge graph allows GPT models to reference realworld entities and their attributes, improving their accuracy and relevance when generating responses. For example, if the model encounters the term "Einstein," it can pull related facts from the knowledge graph about his contributions to physics, enhancing the generated content.

Implementation: To integrate a knowledge graph, developers can utilize APIs to query the graph and retrieve relevant data dynamically. This could involve:

Querying for Entity Information: When the model generates a response involving a specific entity, it can query the knowledge graph to retrieve supplementary information. For instance, if the model discusses "quantum computing," it can look up definitions, applications, and key figures in the field.

Entity Linking: Using techniques to recognize entities within the text and linking them to their counterparts in the knowledge graph. This process helps ensure that the model's responses are anchored in verified data.

3. Utilizing APIs for External Data Sources:

APIs as Knowledge Sources: Many organizations and services provide APIs that grant access to extensive databases and information repositories. Examples include APIs from platforms like Wikipedia, medical databases, and financial data providers.

Dynamic Information Retrieval: By integrating these APIs into the GPT model's workflow, it can query relevant data in real time, allowing it to incorporate uptodate information into its responses. This can be particularly useful for applications requiring current knowledge, such as news generation or customer support.

Implementation Example:

When a user asks a question about the latest advancements in artificial intelligence, the model can query an AIrelated API to gather recent articles, research papers, and summaries, ensuring that the provided information is accurate and current.

4. Contextual Augmentation Techniques:

Augmented Contextualization: This technique involves enriching the input context for the GPT model with information from external knowledge bases. By providing the model with additional context during inference, developers can enhance its understanding of the topic at hand.

Example Techniques:

Prepending Context: Before generating a response, additional relevant facts or data can be prepended to the input prompt. For example, if a user asks about a specific historical event, you can prepend relevant details from a historical database to provide the model with context.

Dynamic Context Creation: Construct dynamic input contexts based on user queries. For example, if a user inquires about "climate change," the model could be provided with current statistics, key figures, and definitions to improve its response quality.

5. Knowledge Base Fusion Techniques:

Combining Multiple Knowledge Sources: Developers can integrate multiple external knowledge bases to create a more comprehensive dataset. By merging information from various sources, the model can leverage a richer context, which can improve its ability to generate accurate responses.

Example of Fusion: In an application focused on medical information, merging data from a medical knowledge graph with information from clinical trials can provide the model with a wellrounded understanding of diseases, treatments, and ongoing research.

6. Embedding External Knowledge:

Using Vector Representations: External knowledge can be transformed into vector representations that can be used alongside the GPT model's embeddings. By encoding knowledge from external sources as vectors, developers can create a seamless integration of domain knowledge into the model's predictions.

RetrievalAugmented Generation (RAG): This technique combines retrieval systems with generative models, allowing the model to access external information while generating text. RAG systems typically retrieve relevant documents or data before generating a response, resulting in more accurate and informed outputs.

7. Evaluation of Knowledge Integration:

Metrics for Assessing Accuracy: When integrating external knowledge bases, it's essential to evaluate how this incorporation impacts the accuracy and relevance of the model's predictions. Metrics like precision, recall, and F1 score can be used to assess performance.

User Feedback and Iteration: Gathering user feedback on the model's responses can help identify areas where external knowledge integration is effective or where improvements are needed. Iterative refinement based on this feedback can enhance the quality of the model's outputs over time.

8. Challenges and Considerations:

Data Quality: The effectiveness of integrating external knowledge depends heavily on the quality of the data sources used. It's essential to select reputable and reliable knowledge bases to ensure that the information retrieved is accurate.

Latency Concerns: Querying external knowledge sources can introduce latency into the response generation process. Balancing the need for uptodate information with response speed is crucial, particularly in applications requiring realtime interaction.

Scalability: As the integration of external knowledge bases increases, it's important to consider the scalability of the system. Ensuring that the architecture can handle an increasing amount of data and queries without sacrificing performance is vital.

By incorporating external knowledge bases and leveraging structured data sources, developers can significantly enhance the capabilities of GPT models. This approach not only improves the accuracy and relevance of the generated content but also enables the model to provide richer, more informed responses that are rooted in verified information. Through careful implementation and ongoing evaluation, the integration of external knowledge can transform GPT models into powerful tools for a wide range of applications across various domains

Chapter 5

Deploying Customized GPT Models

PREPARING THE MODEL FOR DEPLOYMENT

Exporting and Saving Finetuned Models

Deploying customized GPT models effectively requires careful preparation, particularly in terms of exporting and saving the finetuned models. This process ensures that the models can be easily utilized in production environments while maintaining the integrity and performance enhancements achieved during the finetuning process.

1. Model Export Formats:

Understanding Export Formats: Finetuned models can be saved in various formats depending on the framework used (e.g., TensorFlow, PyTorch). Common formats include:

PyTorch Model State Dictionary (`.pt` or `.bin`): This format saves the model weights and architecture, making it easy to load and use later.

TensorFlow SavedModel Format: This format saves the entire model, including weights, architecture, and training configuration, allowing for easier deployment across different environments.

ONNX (Open Neural Network Exchange): A versatile format for sharing models across different frameworks. It allows the model to be run in various environments that support ONNX.

2. Exporting the Model:

Saving the Model in PyTorch:

```python
import torch

Assuming 'model' is your finetuned GPT model

torch.save(model.state_dict(), 'fine_tuned_gpt_model.pt')
```

```
```

Saving the Model in TensorFlow:

```python
model.save('fine_tuned_gpt_model')
```

Using ONNX for Export:

```python
import torch.onnx
```

Convert to ONNX format

```
torch.onnx.export(model,                          dummy_input,
'fine_tuned_gpt_model.onnx')
```

```
```

3. Model Metadata:

Saving Additional Information: Along with the model weights, it is important to save metadata that includes details about the finetuning process, such as:

Training Hyperparameters: Learning rate, batch size, number of epochs, etc.

Dataset Information: The datasets used for finetuning, including any preprocessing steps.

Evaluation Metrics: Performance metrics achieved during finetuning, providing context for future evaluations.

4. Best Practices for Model Versioning and Management:

Version Control Systems: Use version control systems, like Git, to manage changes to model files and ensure that you can revert to previous versions if necessary. This is particularly important in collaborative environments where multiple developers may be working on model improvements.

Model Registry: Implement a model registry to track different versions of your finetuned models. A model registry can help organize models by version, track associated metadata, and facilitate deployment processes. Popular model registry tools include:

MLflow: An opensource platform for managing the machine learning lifecycle, including experimentation, reproducibility, and deployment.

DVC (Data Version Control): A version control system for machine learning projects that allows you to track and manage datasets, models, and code.

Naming Conventions: Establish a consistent naming convention for your models to indicate version numbers, training dates, or specific characteristics. For example, `gpt_model_v1.0_20240810`.

5. Environment Configuration:

Containerization: Use containerization technologies, such as Docker, to encapsulate the model and its dependencies. This ensures that the model runs consistently across different environments and eliminates issues related to dependency management.

Environment Files: Create environment configuration files (e.g., `requirements.txt` for Python) that specify all the libraries and their versions needed to run the model. This helps ensure that any environment where the model is deployed is properly configured.

6. Testing the Exported Model:

Validation of Exported Model: After exporting the model, it is essential to validate that the exported version behaves as expected. This involves loading the model and running a series of test inputs to verify that the outputs match those from the original finetuned model.

```python
Loading the saved model in PyTorch

model = GPTModelClass()

model.load_state_dict(torch.load('fine_tuned_gpt_model.pt'))

model.eval()

Test the model with sample input

test_input = "Sample input text."

output = model(test_input)

print(output)
```

```

```

Performance Comparison: Compare the performance metrics of the exported model with those of the finetuned version to ensure there is no degradation in performance during the export process.

7. Documentation:

Comprehensive Documentation: Document the entire process of exporting and saving the model, including:

Export Steps: Detailed instructions on how to export the model, including code snippets.

Versioning Practices: Guidelines for maintaining and tracking model versions.

Deployment Instructions: Steps for deploying the model in various environments, including any necessary configurations.

8. Backup and Recovery:

Model Backup Strategies: Implement a backup strategy for the exported models to prevent data loss. Regularly back up the model files and associated metadata to secure storage solutions, such as cloud storage services (e.g., AWS S3, Google Cloud Storage).

Disaster Recovery Plan: Develop a disaster recovery plan that outlines the steps to restore the model and its environment in case of failure. This plan should include backup schedules and procedures for restoring the latest version of the model.

By following these steps for exporting, saving, and managing finetuned GPT models, developers can ensure that their customized models are prepared for deployment efficiently and effectively. A wellstructured deployment process not only facilitates smooth integration into production environments but also enhances collaboration and the longterm maintenance of the model. Implementing best practices for versioning and management allows teams to leverage their models confidently and continue refining their performance over time.

DEPLOYMENT STRATEGIES IN PYTHON

Deploying GPT Models in Production Environments

Once a GPT model has been finetuned and prepared for deployment, it is essential to choose the right strategy for making it accessible in production environments. This section discusses various deployment methods, including using REST APIs, cloud platforms, and local servers, outlining their advantages, implementation details, and considerations.

1. Using REST APIs for Deployment:

Overview of REST APIs: REST (Representational State Transfer) APIs provide a standardized way for applications to communicate with each other over the web. By exposing the GPT model through a REST API, developers can make it easily accessible for various client applications, including web apps, mobile apps, and other services.

Frameworks for Creating REST APIs:

Flask: A lightweight web framework for Python that is easy to use for creating simple APIs.

FastAPI: A modern web framework that is built on top of Starlette, known for its high performance and ease of use. FastAPI also supports automatic generation of API documentation.

Example Implementation with Flask:

```python
from flask import Flask, request, jsonify

from your_model import load_model, generate_response

app = Flask(__name__)

Load your finetuned GPT model

model = load_model()

@app.route('/generate', methods=['POST'])

def generate():

    data = request.json

    input_text = data.get('input_text')

    response = generate_response(model, input_text)

    return jsonify({'response': response})

if __name__ == '__main__':

    app.run(host='0.0.0.0', port=5000)
```

Deployment Considerations:

Scaling: As user demand grows, consider deploying your API on platforms that support scaling, such as AWS Elastic Beanstalk or Heroku.

Load Balancing: Implement load balancing strategies to manage traffic effectively, distributing requests across multiple instances of your API.

Security: Ensure proper security measures are in place, such as API keys, rate limiting, and HTTPS, to protect your API from unauthorized access.

2. Deploying on Cloud Platforms:

Advantages of Cloud Deployment: Cloud platforms offer scalability, reliability, and managed services that simplify the deployment process. They allow developers to focus on model performance without worrying about infrastructure management.

Popular Cloud Platforms:

Amazon Web Services (AWS):

Elastic Beanstalk: A Platform as a Service (PaaS) that enables easy deployment of applications. You can deploy your Flask or FastAPI application here.

AWS Lambda: A serverless computing service that allows you to run your code in response to events without provisioning or managing servers.

Google Cloud Platform (GCP):

Google App Engine: A fully managed serverless platform that allows you to deploy applications quickly and scale automatically.

Cloud Run: A serverless platform that runs containers in a fully managed environment, perfect for deploying REST APIs.

Microsoft Azure:

Azure App Service: A fully managed platform for building, deploying, and scaling web apps, including REST APIs.

Example Deployment on AWS Elastic Beanstalk:

Package your application code, including the necessary dependencies in a `requirements.txt` file, and deploy it using the Elastic Beanstalk console or CLI.

Configure the environment variables and resource settings through the Elastic Beanstalk dashboard.

3. Local Server Deployment:

When to Use Local Servers: For development, testing, or smallscale applications, deploying the GPT model on a local server may be sufficient. Local servers allow for direct control over the environment and are costeffective.

Setting Up a Local Server:

Use a framework like Flask or FastAPI to create an API that serves your model locally.

Install dependencies and configure the server environment. Ensure that the necessary hardware and software are set up to handle the expected load.

Example for running a Flask application locally:

```bash
```

```
Install dependencies

pip install Flask your_model_library

Run the application

python your_flask_app.py
```
```

Considerations for Local Deployment:

Resource Management: Ensure that your local server has sufficient resources (CPU, memory) to handle inference requests, especially if expecting high usage.

Networking: Configure your local server's network settings to allow access from client applications, including any necessary firewall or routing adjustments.

Limited Scalability: Keep in mind that local deployments may struggle to scale as demand increases, unlike cloudbased solutions.

4. Containerization for Deployment:
```

Using Docker for Containerization: Docker allows developers to package applications and their dependencies into containers, ensuring that they run consistently across different environments.

Benefits of Containerization:

Isolation: Containers provide isolated environments, preventing conflicts with other applications.

Portability: Docker images can be deployed across various platforms and cloud services easily.

Creating a Dockerfile for Your Model:

```dockerfile
FROM python:3.8slim

WORKDIR /app

 Copy the application code

COPY . .

 Install dependencies

RUN pip install r requirements.txt
```

Expose the port for the API

EXPOSE 5000

Command to run the application

CMD ["python", "your_flask_app.py"]

```
```

Running the Container:

```bash
```

Build the Docker image

docker build t gpt_model_api .

Run the Docker container

docker run p 5000:5000 gpt_model_api

```
```

5. Monitoring and Maintenance:

Performance Monitoring: Implement monitoring solutions to track the performance of your deployed model, such as request response times, error rates, and server resource utilization.

Logging: Use logging frameworks to log API requests, responses, and any errors that occur during execution. This helps in debugging and performance analysis.

Continuous Deployment: Set up continuous integration and deployment (CI/CD) pipelines to automate the deployment process, allowing for rapid updates and improvements to the model.

6. User Feedback and Iteration:

Collecting User Feedback: After deployment, gather feedback from users regarding the performance and usability of the model. This feedback is essential for identifying areas for improvement.

Iterative Updates: Use the collected feedback to refine and update the model periodically, ensuring it continues to meet user needs and expectations.

By employing these deployment strategies, developers can ensure that their customized GPT models are effectively deployed in production environments. Whether using REST APIs, cloud platforms, local servers, or containerization, it is essential to consider factors such as scalability, security, monitoring, and user feedback to maintain and improve the model's performance over time. With the right deployment strategy in place, organizations can leverage the capabilities of GPT models to provide valuable services and solutions to their users.

PERFORMANCE OPTIMIZATION IN REALTIME APPLICATIONS

In realtime applications, the performance of customized GPT models is critical, as users expect quick and accurate responses. This section explores techniques for optimizing model performance, focusing on reducing latency and resource consumption, as well as balancing accuracy and performance in highdemand scenarios.

1. Techniques for Reducing Latency and Resource Consumption:

Model Compression:

Quantization: This technique reduces the precision of the model's weights from floatingpoint to lowerbit representations (e.g., INT8), which can significantly decrease the model size and improve inference speed without substantial loss in accuracy.

Pruning: Pruning involves removing less important neurons or weights from the model, leading to a smaller and faster model.

This can be done through techniques like weight pruning (removing weights below a certain threshold) or neuron pruning (removing entire neurons based on their contribution to the model's performance).

Knowledge Distillation: This approach involves training a smaller "student" model to mimic a larger, more complex "teacher" model. The student model learns to approximate the teacher's predictions, resulting in a more lightweight model that can deliver fast responses with minimal accuracy loss.

Batch Processing:

Batched Inference: Instead of processing requests one at a time, batch multiple inputs together and process them simultaneously. This can improve throughput and reduce the overall latency per request by taking advantage of parallel processing capabilities.

Asynchronous Processing: Implementing asynchronous processing allows the server to handle incoming requests while waiting for responses from the model. This can improve overall responsiveness and user experience.

Optimizing Inference Pipeline:

Reducing Input Size: Limit the length of input sequences to only the most relevant information. For example, truncating text inputs can speed up processing time without significantly impacting the model's effectiveness.

Caching Mechanisms: Utilize caching to store frequently requested outputs. By returning cached results for repeated queries, latency can be dramatically reduced for commonly used inputs.

Edge Computing: Deploy the model closer to the user by using edge computing. By processing requests on local servers or devices instead of a centralized cloud server, latency can be minimized, especially in applications requiring realtime responsiveness.

2. Balancing Accuracy and Performance in HighDemand Scenarios:

Adaptive Inference Strategies:

Dynamic Model Selection: Implement adaptive algorithms that select different models based on the current demand and complexity of the task. For instance, use a lightweight model for simpler queries and a more complex model for detailed requests. This ensures that performance is optimized based on the context.

Quality of Service (QoS) Levels: Define different QoS levels for responses, allowing users to choose between faster responses with slightly lower accuracy or more detailed responses with higher latency. This gives users control over their experience and helps balance performance demands.

Regularization Techniques:

Dropout: Implement dropout during training to prevent overfitting. This can improve generalization, allowing the model to maintain high performance even in dynamic conditions with varying input types.

Data Augmentation: Use data augmentation techniques during training to expose the model to a broader range of scenarios. This can enhance the model's robustness and help maintain accuracy in realtime applications where input data can vary significantly.

Monitoring and Adjusting Inference Settings:

RealTime Performance Monitoring: Continuously monitor model performance metrics in real time, such as latency and accuracy. Set up alerts for when performance degrades, allowing for timely interventions or model adjustments.

Feedback Loops: Implement mechanisms to collect user feedback on response quality. Use this feedback to adjust the model parameters or inference strategies dynamically, ensuring that user satisfaction remains high while performance is optimized.

3. Hardware Optimization:

Utilizing GPUs and TPUs: Leverage hardware accelerators such as Graphics Processing Units (GPUs) or Tensor Processing Units (TPUs) that are optimized for machine learning tasks. These can significantly reduce inference time compared to traditional CPUbased processing.

Model Deployment on Specialized Hardware: Consider deploying the model on specialized hardware, such as FPGAs (FieldProgrammable Gate Arrays) or ASICs (ApplicationSpecific Integrated Circuits), which can be optimized for specific inference tasks. This can provide considerable speedups in realtime applications.

4. User Experience Considerations:

Progressive Loading: Implement progressive loading techniques where an initial response is provided quickly, followed by more detailed information as it becomes available. This approach can enhance user experience by providing immediate feedback while allowing the model to process complex queries in the background.

Personalization: Tailor responses based on user preferences or previous interactions. Personalized responses can improve user satisfaction and perception of model performance, allowing for a balance between quick responses and content relevance.

5. Continuous Performance Improvement:

A/B Testing: Conduct A/B testing to evaluate different model configurations and deployment strategies in realtime. This allows for datadriven decisions on which approaches provide the best balance of accuracy and performance.

Iterative Refinement: Continuously refine the model and deployment strategies based on performance metrics and user feedback. Regular updates and adjustments can ensure that the model remains effective even as demand and user expectations evolve.

By implementing these performance optimization techniques, developers can ensure that their customized GPT models deliver fast, accurate responses even in highdemand scenarios. Balancing latency and resource consumption with accuracy is crucial for maintaining user satisfaction and maximizing the model's value in realtime applications. Through continuous monitoring, adaptive strategies, and leveraging appropriate hardware, organizations can achieve optimal performance while meeting the evolving needs of their users.

Chapter 6

Challenges and Best Practices in Customizing GPT Models

ADDRESSING COMMON CHALLENGES IN FINETUNING

Finetuning GPT models for specific applications can be challenging due to various factors, including overfitting, data scarcity, and model biases. This section discusses these common challenges and offers strategies for mitigating these issues to ensure effective customization of GPT models.

1. Overfitting:

Understanding Overfitting: Overfitting occurs when a model learns the noise and details in the training data to the extent that it negatively impacts its performance on new, unseen data. This results in high accuracy on training data but poor generalization to realworld applications.

Signs of Overfitting:

Discrepancies between training and validation performance, with high training accuracy and significantly lower validation accuracy.

The model performs well on the training dataset but struggles with realworld or test data.

Strategies to Mitigate Overfitting:

Use Regularization Techniques: Incorporate regularization methods such as L1 (Lasso) or L2 (Ridge) regularization, which penalize large weights in the model. This encourages simpler models that generalize better.

Early Stopping: Monitor the model's performance on a validation set during training, and stop training when performance starts to degrade. This helps prevent the model from learning unnecessary patterns that lead to overfitting.

CrossValidation: Utilize crossvalidation techniques to ensure that the model's performance is robust across different subsets of data. This helps in understanding the model's generalization capabilities.

Data Augmentation: Expand the training dataset artificially by creating variations of existing data (e.g., synonym replacement, backtranslation, or paraphrasing). This increases the diversity of the training data and reduces the likelihood of overfitting.

2. Data Scarcity:

Understanding Data Scarcity: Data scarcity refers to the lack of sufficient or highquality training data for specific tasks. This is a common issue when finetuning models for niche applications or domains with limited publicly available data.

Consequences of Data Scarcity:

Inadequate training data can lead to poor model performance, as the model may not learn relevant patterns or context for the specific task.

Limited exposure to diverse examples can result in biased or incomplete model behavior.

Strategies to Address Data Scarcity:

Transfer Learning: Leverage pretrained models that have been trained on large, diverse datasets. Finetuning these models on smaller, domainspecific datasets allows the model to benefit from previously learned knowledge while adapting to the new task.

Synthetic Data Generation: Use data synthesis techniques to create artificial training samples. This can include generating text based on certain templates, simulating conversations, or utilizing generative models to create realistic examples.

Active Learning: Implement active learning strategies where the model is iteratively trained on the most informative samples. By selecting data points that the model is uncertain about, you can efficiently use the limited data available to improve model performance.

Crowdsourcing Data: Consider utilizing crowdsourcing platforms to gather labeled data from a diverse group of contributors. This can help in acquiring more data points while ensuring a variety of perspectives and examples.

3. Model Biases:

Understanding Model Biases: Model biases occur when the model produces outputs that are systematically skewed or unfair due to biases present in the training data. This can lead to undesirable or harmful outcomes in applications, especially those involving sensitive topics.

Types of Biases:

Data Bias: Biases in the training dataset that can stem from unbalanced representation, societal biases, or historical inequities.

Algorithmic Bias: Biases introduced by the model's architecture or training process, which can amplify existing biases in the data.

Strategies for Mitigating Model Biases:

Bias Detection and Evaluation: Regularly evaluate the model for biases by testing it on diverse datasets that encompass a range of demographic groups, contexts, and scenarios. Tools and frameworks are available to measure bias across multiple axes (e.g., gender, ethnicity).

Diversifying Training Data: Ensure that the training dataset is diverse and representative of different groups, perspectives, and contexts. Actively seek out underrepresented data points to create a more balanced training set.

Incorporating Fairness Constraints: Implement fairness constraints during the training process to ensure that the model does not favor specific groups or demographics. This can include adjusting loss functions to account for fairness metrics.

PostProcessing Adjustments: Apply techniques after training to adjust the model's outputs to reduce biases. This can involve modifying the output distribution to promote fairness in the generated text.

4. Continuous Learning and Adaptation:

Feedback Mechanisms: Establish feedback loops to continuously collect user input and model performance data. This information can inform ongoing adjustments and refinements to the model.

Regular Updates: Regularly update the model based on new data and user feedback. This ensures that the model remains relevant and effective in a dynamic environment.

5. Documentation and Collaboration:

Comprehensive Documentation: Maintain thorough documentation of the data sources, training processes, biases detected, and the strategies implemented to mitigate them. This transparency supports future development and ethical considerations.

Collaborative Development: Engage with interdisciplinary teams that include domain experts, ethicists, and data scientists to ensure a wellrounded approach to finetuning and mitigating challenges in customizing GPT models.

By understanding and addressing the common challenges associated with finetuning GPT models, developers can create more robust and effective customized solutions. Implementing these strategies can enhance model performance, reduce biases, and ensure that the customized models deliver valuable outputs in realworld applications.

ETHICAL CONSIDERATIONS IN MODEL CUSTOMIZATION

As GPT models are increasingly adopted for various applications, it is crucial to address ethical considerations during the customization process. This section focuses on ensuring fairness, avoiding harmful biases, and establishing guidelines for the ethical use of customized GPT models.

1. Ensuring Fairness and Avoiding Harmful Biases:

Understanding Bias in AI Models:

Bias in AI can emerge from multiple sources, including the data used for training, the design of the model, and the context in which it is applied. Bias can lead to unfair treatment of individuals or groups, perpetuating stereotypes and discrimination.

Common types of biases include gender bias, racial bias, socioeconomic bias, and more. These biases can significantly impact the quality and fairness of the outputs generated by the model.

Techniques for Identifying Bias:

Diverse Testing Datasets: To evaluate bias in customized models, use diverse testing datasets that reflect various demographic groups and scenarios. This helps identify potential biases in the model's outputs.

Bias Metrics: Implement bias detection tools and metrics to quantify the degree of bias present in the model's predictions. These metrics can include demographic parity, equal opportunity, and disparate impact.

Strategies to Mitigate Bias:

Balanced Training Data: Ensure that the training dataset is representative of different groups and perspectives. Actively seek out underrepresented data points to create a more balanced dataset.

Bias Correction Techniques: Utilize techniques such as adversarial debiasing, where the model is trained to minimize bias while maintaining predictive accuracy. This involves training the model with fairness constraints to prevent it from learning biased patterns.

Human Oversight: Involve domain experts and ethicists in the model development process to provide insights on potential biases and ensure that the model aligns with ethical standards.

2. Guidelines for Ethical Use of Customized GPT Models:

Transparency and Explainability:

Model Documentation: Maintain comprehensive documentation of the model's architecture, training data, and customization processes. Transparency regarding how the model was developed and the data used helps stakeholders understand its capabilities and limitations.

Explainable AI: Implement techniques that provide explanations for the model's outputs. Explainability helps users understand the reasoning behind generated responses, fostering trust and accountability.

User Consent and Data Privacy:

Informed Consent: Obtain informed consent from users when collecting and using their data for model training or finetuning. Clearly communicate how their data will be used and the potential risks involved.

Data Privacy Measures: Implement robust data privacy practices to safeguard user information. This includes anonymizing data, encrypting sensitive information, and adhering to relevant data protection regulations (e.g., GDPR, CCPA).

Preventing Misuse of Models:

Use Case Restrictions: Clearly define the intended use cases for customized models and implement restrictions to prevent misuse. For example, avoid deploying models in contexts where they could perpetuate harm or spread misinformation.

Monitoring Model Outputs: Continuously monitor the outputs generated by the model to identify and address any harmful or unethical content. This proactive approach helps mitigate risks associated with model misuse.

Ethical Review Boards:

Establishing Ethics Committees: Create interdisciplinary ethics review boards to evaluate model development and deployment processes. These committees can provide guidance on ethical considerations and ensure compliance with ethical standards.

Regular Ethical Audits: Conduct regular audits of the model's performance and its societal impacts. Assess the model's compliance with ethical guidelines and make adjustments as necessary.

3. Promoting Inclusivity and Fair Access:

Inclusive Development Practices: Engage with diverse communities and stakeholders throughout the model development process. Their insights can help identify potential biases and enhance the model's relevance and applicability.

Access to Technology: Ensure equitable access to customized models across different communities and demographics. Consider providing resources and support to underrepresented groups to empower them to leverage AI technologies.

4. Fostering a Culture of Ethical AI:

Training and Awareness: Provide training for developers, data scientists, and stakeholders on ethical AI practices and the importance of fairness and inclusivity. Cultivating awareness fosters a culture of responsibility and ethical considerations in AI development.

Encouraging Open Dialogue: Promote open discussions around ethical considerations in AI. Encourage feedback and suggestions from users, experts, and communities to continuously improve ethical practices.

By prioritizing ethical considerations during the customization of GPT models, developers can create solutions that are not only effective but also fair and responsible. Addressing biases, ensuring transparency, and adhering to ethical guidelines will help build trust in AI technologies while promoting their positive societal impact.

BEST PRACTICES FOR LONGTERM MODEL MAINTENANCE

To ensure the continued effectiveness and relevance of customized GPT models, it is essential to implement best practices for longterm maintenance. This section focuses on monitoring model performance over time and the necessity of updating and retraining models as needed.

1. Monitoring Model Performance Over Time:

Establishing Key Performance Indicators (KPIs):

Define specific KPIs to assess the model's performance in realworld applications. Common KPIs for GPT models may include accuracy, response relevance, user satisfaction scores, and engagement metrics.

Continuously track these KPIs to identify any performance degradation or shifts in user needs and preferences.

Continuous Evaluation:

Implement ongoing evaluation processes to regularly assess the model's performance on diverse datasets. This helps detect any biases or inaccuracies that may arise as the model interacts with users over time.

Use a combination of automated testing and user feedback to evaluate model performance in various contexts and applications.

Feedback Mechanisms:

Create channels for users to provide feedback on the model's outputs. This feedback can offer valuable insights into the model's strengths and weaknesses and inform necessary adjustments.

Regularly analyze user feedback to identify patterns and areas for improvement. User sentiment analysis can provide deeper insights into how well the model is meeting user expectations.

Alert Systems:

Set up alert systems to notify developers when performance metrics fall below predetermined thresholds. This proactive approach allows for timely interventions to address performance issues.

2. Updating and Retraining Models as Needed:

Data Drift and Concept Drift:

Recognize that the data distribution and underlying patterns may change over time (data drift) or that the context of the task may evolve (concept drift). This can affect the model's accuracy and relevance.

Regularly review the training data and update it to reflect any changes in user behavior, preferences, or societal norms.

Retraining Strategies:

Scheduled Retraining: Establish a schedule for periodic retraining of the model using updated data. Depending on the application, this could be done quarterly, biannually, or annually.

Incremental Learning: Consider implementing incremental learning approaches, where the model is updated with new data without requiring a complete retraining from scratch. This can be more efficient and save computational resources.

Transfer Learning for Updates: Utilize transfer learning techniques to leverage knowledge from existing models when incorporating new data. This can enhance the efficiency of the retraining process.

Testing and Validation:

Before deploying updated models, conduct rigorous testing and validation to ensure that improvements have been made without introducing new issues. This includes evaluating performance on both training and validation datasets.

Employ A/B testing to compare the performance of the updated model against the existing one in a controlled environment. Analyze user interactions and engagement to determine the effectiveness of the updates.

3. Documenting Changes and Version Control:

Model Versioning: Implement a version control system to track changes made to the model, including updates to training data, architecture modifications, and finetuning processes. This documentation is critical for transparency and accountability.

Change Logs: Maintain comprehensive change logs detailing the reasons for updates, the data used, and any performance metrics associated with previous versions. This helps in assessing the impact of changes over time.

4. Collaboration and Knowledge Sharing:

CrossFunctional Collaboration: Foster collaboration between data scientists, developers, and domain experts to share insights and knowledge on model performance and necessary updates. Interdisciplinary teams can identify potential issues more effectively.

Community Engagement: Engage with user communities and stakeholders to gather insights on how the model is being used and any emerging needs. Their feedback can guide future updates and enhancements.

5. Ethical Considerations in Model Updates:

Bias and Fairness Review: Regularly review updated models for biases and ensure that fairness considerations are integrated into the retraining process. This is critical for maintaining trust and integrity in the model's outputs.

Transparency in Changes: Communicate any significant updates or changes to users, along with the rationale behind these modifications. Transparency builds trust and encourages user engagement.

By implementing these best practices for longterm model maintenance, developers can ensure that customized GPT models remain effective, accurate, and relevant over time. Continuous monitoring, timely updates, and user engagement are essential to adapting to evolving needs and maintaining the quality of AIdriven solutions.

Chapter 7

Conclusion and Future Directions

SUMMARY OF KEY TAKEAWAYS

This chapter concludes the discussion on optimizing performance through finetuning and customizing GPT models in Python. It recaps the essential aspects of customization, highlights the lessons learned throughout the process, and considers future directions for the field.

1. Recap of the Importance of FineTuning and Customization:

Tailoring Models to Specific Needs:

Finetuning and customizing GPT models allow developers to tailor the models to meet specific application needs and user requirements. This process enhances the model's relevance and effectiveness, resulting in better user experiences and outcomes.

Customized models can address domainspecific language, cultural nuances, and specialized tasks that generalpurpose models may not adequately handle.

Improving Accuracy and Performance:

Through finetuning, developers can significantly enhance the accuracy and performance of GPT models. By training on highquality, domainspecific datasets, models can better understand context, generate more relevant responses, and reduce errors.

The process of customization also enables the incorporation of external knowledge bases, improving the model's ability to provide informed and contextually aware responses.

Addressing Ethical Considerations:

Customization efforts must be accompanied by a strong emphasis on ethical considerations. Addressing biases, ensuring fairness, and maintaining transparency are critical components of responsible AI development.

Implementing best practices for ethical AI use helps build trust among users and ensures that customized models contribute positively to society.

2. Key Lessons Learned from Optimizing GPT Models:

Importance of Data Quality:

The quality of training data plays a crucial role in the success of finetuning efforts. Highquality, diverse, and representative datasets lead to better model performance and reduced biases. Regular reviews and updates to training data are essential to maintaining relevance and accuracy.

Iterative Improvement Process:

Finetuning and customization is an iterative process that requires ongoing evaluation and refinement. Continuous monitoring, user feedback, and performance analysis are vital for identifying areas for improvement and ensuring that models remain effective over time.

Collaboration and Knowledge Sharing:

Crossfunctional collaboration among developers, domain experts, and stakeholders enhances the customization process.

Sharing knowledge and insights can lead to innovative solutions and a deeper understanding of user needs.

Adaptability to Change:

The landscape of AI and natural language processing is constantly evolving. Developers must remain adaptable and open to incorporating new techniques, technologies, and ethical considerations into their customization strategies.

3. Future Directions for GPT Model Customization:

Advancements in Model Architecture:

As research in natural language processing continues, future directions may include exploring novel architectures and methodologies for GPT models. These advancements could lead to improved performance, reduced biases, and enhanced capabilities for understanding complex contexts.

Integration with Emerging Technologies:

The integration of GPT models with other emerging technologies, such as reinforcement learning, can offer new opportunities for enhancing model performance and interactivity.

This hybrid approach may lead to more dynamic and responsive AI systems.

Focus on Explainability and Interpretability:

Future efforts should prioritize the development of models that are not only accurate but also interpretable and explainable. Ensuring that users can understand how decisions are made will foster trust and confidence in AI systems.

Ethical Standards and Regulations:

As AI technologies become more prevalent, the establishment of ethical standards and regulations will be crucial. Collaborating with policymakers, ethicists, and industry stakeholders can help shape a responsible framework for the use of customized AI models.

Community Engagement and Collaboration:

Engaging with user communities and fostering collaboration will be essential for identifying realworld challenges and opportunities in model customization. Inclusive development practices can lead to solutions that are more equitable and beneficial to diverse user groups.

In summary, the journey of finetuning and customizing GPT models in Python is an ongoing process that involves continuous learning, adaptation, and collaboration. By applying the lessons learned and embracing future directions, developers can contribute to creating more effective, responsible, and innovative AI solutions that meet the evolving needs of users and society.

ENCOURAGEMENT FOR CONTINUED EXPLORATION

As we conclude this exploration of optimizing performance through finetuning and customizing GPT models in Python, it is essential to inspire readers to continue their journey in this dynamic field. This section encourages experimentation with advanced customization techniques and provides resources for further learning and development.

1. Encouragement to Experiment with Advanced Customization Techniques:

Embrace a Learning Mindset:

The field of artificial intelligence and natural language processing is continuously evolving, and staying updated with the latest trends and techniques is crucial. Embrace a mindset of lifelong learning to remain adaptable and innovative in your approach to customizing GPT models.

Experimenting with different finetuning strategies, tokenization methods, and model architectures can lead to new insights and breakthroughs. Don't hesitate to try unconventional approaches, as they may yield unexpected benefits.

Utilize RealWorld Projects:

Apply your knowledge by working on realworld projects that involve customizing GPT models. Engaging in practical applications allows you to gain handson experience and develop a deeper understanding of the challenges and intricacies of model customization.

Consider collaborating with peers or joining opensource projects to broaden your exposure and contribute to communitydriven initiatives. This collaborative spirit fosters innovation and the sharing of best practices.

Set Goals for Customization:

Define specific goals for your customization efforts, whether they involve improving accuracy for a particular application, reducing biases, or enhancing user experience. Setting clear objectives can guide your experimentation and provide motivation as you work towards achieving meaningful outcomes.

Monitor your progress and celebrate your achievements, no matter how small. Each successful customization effort contributes to your growth as a developer and enhances your understanding of GPT models.

2. Resources for Further Learning and Development:

Online Courses and Tutorials:

Numerous online platforms offer courses focused on natural language processing, deep learning, and GPT model customization. Websites like Coursera, edX, and Udacity provide access to courses taught by industry experts that cover essential concepts and practical applications.

Explore tutorials and guides available on platforms like Medium and Towards Data Science, where practitioners share their experiences and insights on customizing GPT models.

Books and Research Papers:

Consider reading books dedicated to natural language processing and AI development. Titles like "Deep Learning for Natural Language Processing" and "HandsOn Machine Learning with ScikitLearn, Keras, and TensorFlow" can provide valuable theoretical knowledge and practical tips.

Stay updated with the latest research papers published in AI conferences and journals. Websites like arXiv.org and Google Scholar are excellent resources for accessing cuttingedge research and insights into the latest advancements in GPT models and their applications.

Community Engagement:

Join online communities and forums where AI practitioners gather to share knowledge, ask questions, and collaborate on projects. Platforms like Reddit, Stack Overflow, and specialized Discord servers can provide valuable support and networking opportunities.

Participate in hackathons, webinars, and workshops focused on GPT and natural language processing. These events can offer practical insights, expose you to new tools, and connect you with fellow enthusiasts and experts in the field.

Documentation and Official Resources:

Familiarize yourself with the official documentation provided by OpenAI and other libraries related to GPT models. Understanding the functionalities and parameters of various libraries, such as Hugging Face Transformers, is essential for effective model customization.

Utilize GitHub repositories to explore opensource projects that focus on GPT customization. Examining code examples and best practices shared by the community can provide inspiration and practical solutions to common challenges.

By encouraging continued exploration and providing access to valuable resources, readers can build upon their knowledge and skills in customizing GPT models. This journey promises exciting opportunities for innovation, collaboration, and contribution to the evolving landscape of AI. As you embark on this path, remember that each experiment and every project brings you closer to mastering the art of optimizing performance in GPT models.

THE FUTURE OF GPT CUSTOMIZATION IN PYTHON

*As we look toward the future of GPT customization in Python, it is essential to consider the emerging trends and technologies that will shape the landscape of artificial intelligence (AI) and its applications. This section discusses the anticipated advancements in GPT customization and provides predictions for the future of AIdriven applications and models.

1. Emerging Trends and Technologies in GPT Customization:

Advancements in Model Architectures:

The architecture of GPT models is likely to evolve significantly, incorporating new innovations that enhance performance and efficiency. Future models may adopt hybrid architectures that combine the strengths of transformerbased models with other methodologies, such as recurrent neural networks (RNNs) or convolutional neural networks (CNNs).

Research into sparse attention mechanisms and efficient transformers is gaining traction, potentially leading to models that can handle larger contexts with lower computational costs, allowing for even more sophisticated customization.

Increased Focus on Multimodal Models:

Future GPT models may increasingly integrate multimodal capabilities, allowing them to process and generate text, images, audio, and video simultaneously. This shift toward multimodal AI can create richer and more interactive applications, enhancing user experiences across various domains.

Customization efforts will need to adapt to these multimodal environments, focusing on how to leverage diverse data sources to create comprehensive AI solutions tailored to specific use cases.

Integration of Continual Learning Techniques:

The concept of continual learning, where models adapt and learn from new data over time without forgetting previous knowledge, is becoming increasingly relevant. Future customization efforts may incorporate techniques that allow GPT models to continually update their knowledge bases and improve performance as they interact with users and receive feedback.

This approach could lead to more dynamic and responsive AI applications, as models can adapt to changing user needs and evolving contexts.

Emphasis on Explainability and Transparency:

As the use of AI in critical applications grows, there will be a heightened focus on explainability and transparency in GPT customization. Developers will need to implement techniques that enhance model interpretability, allowing users to understand the reasoning behind AIgenerated responses.

Future tools and libraries may prioritize features that facilitate explainability, helping users identify biases and ensuring that customized models adhere to ethical standards.

2. Predictions for the Future of AIDriven Applications and Models:

Widespread Adoption Across Industries:

GPT models will likely see widespread adoption across various industries, including healthcare, finance, education, and entertainment. Customized AI solutions will become integral to enhancing customer experiences, streamlining operations, and providing valuable insights based on data analysis.

As businesses increasingly recognize the potential of AIdriven applications, demand for skilled developers proficient in customizing GPT models will grow, leading to a more competitive landscape in AI talent.

Personalized User Experiences:

The future of AIdriven applications will prioritize personalization, with customized GPT models capable of tailoring interactions based on individual user preferences, behaviors, and contexts. This shift will enhance user engagement and satisfaction, making AI tools more intuitive and relevant to specific audiences.

As models become more adept at understanding context and user intent, businesses can create targeted marketing strategies and personalized recommendations, fostering deeper connections with customers.

AIPowered Automation and DecisionMaking:

The integration of GPT models into business processes will drive automation and datadriven decisionmaking. Customized AI systems will empower organizations to analyze vast amounts of data quickly, identify trends, and generate actionable insights, ultimately improving operational efficiency and strategic planning.

As AIdriven automation becomes more prevalent, businesses may rely on customized models to assist in complex decisionmaking processes, further solidifying the role of AI as a trusted partner in achieving organizational goals.

Collaboration Between Humans and AI:

The future will likely see a harmonious collaboration between humans and AI, with GPT models acting as tools to augment human capabilities rather than replace them. Customized models will support professionals in various fields, enhancing creativity, problemsolving, and decisionmaking processes.

This collaborative approach will foster innovation, as human expertise combined with AI capabilities can lead to groundbreaking solutions and advancements in multiple domains.

In summary, the future of GPT customization in Python is poised for exciting developments driven by advancements in technology and a growing understanding of user needs. As developers embrace emerging trends and leverage the power of AIdriven applications, they will play a crucial role in shaping the future of intelligent systems. By remaining adaptable and open to new possibilities, developers can contribute to creating innovative, responsible, and impactful AI solutions that enhance the human experience.

Chapter 10

Conclusion

As we conclude this exploration of optimizing performance through finetuning and customizing GPT models in Python, it is essential to reflect on the key insights and lessons learned throughout this journey. The rapid advancements in artificial intelligence and natural language processing have opened up a world of possibilities for developers, researchers, and organizations. This chapter summarizes the key takeaways, encourages ongoing exploration in the field, and offers final thoughts on the future of GPT customization.

1. Recap of Key Takeaways:

Importance of FineTuning and Customization:

Finetuning and customizing GPT models are crucial for tailoring AI solutions to specific tasks and applications. By leveraging domainspecific data and adjusting hyperparameters, developers can significantly enhance the performance, accuracy, and relevance of their models.

The customization process allows organizations to create AI applications that meet their unique needs, whether in customer service, content generation, or specialized industry solutions.

Techniques and Best Practices:

Throughout the chapters, we have explored various techniques for finetuning and customizing GPT models, including data preparation, model evaluation, and advanced customization strategies. Understanding these practices equips developers with the tools necessary to optimize their models effectively.

Addressing challenges such as overfitting, biases, and ethical considerations is essential for building robust and trustworthy AI systems. By adhering to best practices, developers can create models that not only perform well but also align with societal values and standards.

Future Directions and Opportunities:

The future of GPT customization holds exciting prospects, with advancements in model architectures, the integration of multimodal capabilities, and a focus on explainability and continual learning. Developers are encouraged to stay informed about emerging trends and actively engage in the AI community to share knowledge and collaborate on innovative projects.

As AI continues to evolve, there will be increasing demand for customized solutions across various industries. Developers who embrace continuous learning and experimentation will be wellpositioned to lead in this dynamic landscape.

2. Encouragement for Continued Exploration:

The journey of customizing GPT models is just beginning. Developers are encouraged to experiment with advanced techniques, explore new applications, and seek opportunities for collaboration. Engaging with realworld projects can provide invaluable experience and foster innovation.

Resources for further learning, including online courses, research papers, and community engagement, will empower developers to enhance their skills and stay at the forefront of AI advancements. Embracing a mindset of curiosity and exploration will lead to personal growth and contribute to the ongoing evolution of AI.

3. Final Thoughts on the Evolving Landscape of GPT Customization:

The field of AI is characterized by rapid change and innovation. As GPT models continue to improve, their potential to transform industries and enhance human experiences will only increase. Developers play a crucial role in shaping this future by customizing models that align with user needs and ethical considerations.

The collaboration between humans and AI will define the next era of technology. Customized GPT models will serve as powerful tools to augment human capabilities, enabling more efficient processes, deeper insights, and enriched interactions across various domains.

As we move forward, let us embrace the challenges and opportunities presented by GPT customization, fostering a culture of responsible innovation that prioritizes user needs, transparency, and fairness. Together, we can harness the power of AI to create solutions that positively impact society and improve the quality of life for all.

In conclusion, the journey of customizing GPT models in Python is filled with potential for creativity, innovation, and meaningful contributions to the field of artificial intelligence. By embracing the insights and practices outlined in this work, developers can navigate this exciting landscape and play a vital role in shaping the future of AIdriven applications.